ADVANCED FIBONACCI TRADING

A Price Action Approach To Trend Trading With Fibonacci

Frank Miller

TABLE OF CONTENTS

INTRODUCTION

There are thousands of tools in trading. Yet very few have stood the test of time and remained as widely used as Fibonacci.

From beginners entering the market for the first time to seasoned professional traders, Fibonacci almost always appears somewhere on their charts. Fibonacci levels, Fibonacci retracement zones, and the well-known golden ratios have become an integral part of modern technical analysis. However, despite its widespread popularity, most traders still struggle to turn Fibonacci into a tool that delivers truly effective and consistent results.

Fibonacci levels themselves possess no inherent "magic." They are merely potential price areas — zones where the market is more likely to react with greater intensity than usual. What truly matters is not the fact that price reaches a Fibonacci level, but how the market behaves as it moves into those areas.

The longer I traded, the more I realized that markets are not driven by numbers alone — they are driven by people.

Behind every candle lies fear, greed, hesitation, exhaustion, and the ongoing battle for control between Bulls and Bears. Every price zone is a battlefield. Every period of consolidation reflects a phase where both sides are gradually wearing each other down. And every genuinely powerful breakout or reversal tends to emerge only when one side begins to lose momentum while the other steadily gains control.

That realization became the foundation of this book.

Instead of using Fibonacci as nothing more than a line-drawing tool, we will use it as a framework for identifying price areas worth monitoring, then read price action to determine when the market is genuinely offering us an edge.

Throughout this book, you will notice that the strategies focus heavily on:

- The ongoing struggle between buyers and sellers,
- Multi-top and multi-bottom structures,
- Price compression zones,
- Breakouts,
- Reversal candlestick patterns,
- The process through which market control shifts from one side to the other.

My goal is not to create overly complex strategies filled with indicators cluttering the chart. On the contrary, I want to keep everything sufficiently minimalistic so that you can read the market more clearly, backtest with confidence, verify the logic yourself, and apply it effectively in real trading conditions.

If you have previously read *Secrets on Fibonacci Trading*, you will notice that this book carries a more minimalist and cautious approach, while at the same time exploring far deeper into the logic behind each entry and the way markets truly move.

Beyond entry strategies, this book also dedicates an important section to take profit techniques and trade management — which I believe represent the other half of trading, and often the most difficult half as well. After all, even the best entry strategy becomes meaningless if you do not know how to manage your position and protect your profits.

One final note before we begin: every strategy and example presented throughout this book is explained within the context of an uptrend. Downtrends operate according to the exact same principles, simply mirrored in the opposite direction. In addition, this book is written for traders who already possess a foundational understanding of Fibonacci. If you are still unfamiliar with the tool, I strongly encourage you to begin with *Secrets on Fibonacci Trading* before moving on to the more advanced concepts explored here.

And now, if you are ready, let us begin the journey of reading the market through the lens of Fibonacci, price action, and the ongoing battle between Bulls and Bears.

CHAPTER 1: THE TIMELESS NATURE OF THE MARKET

Leaves on the Water

There is one morning I will never forget.

It was around 6:30 a.m. I was sitting beside a small stream behind a friend's house in the countryside, holding a cup of coffee that was still warm in my hands while watching dry leaves fall from the trees onto the surface of the water.

The moment each leaf touched the stream, it seemed to begin a journey of its own.

Some remained stuck near the edge, caught in patches of moss and unable to go anywhere. Some spun endlessly inside small pockets of swirling water — active and chaotic on the surface, yet never truly making progress. Others drifted into stagnant corners where the current no longer flowed, resting there quietly as time slowly wore them away.

But there were also leaves that settled directly into the center of the current, allowing the water to carry them naturally downstream. They moved through every bend in the stream with a strange sense of ease before eventually disappearing beyond the curve in the distance.

And at that moment, I realized that financial markets are not so different from that stream.

The market is not a competition. It is not a battle, nor is it a perfectly rational machine that rewards people according to their intelligence, discipline, or effort. At its deepest level, the market resembles a river more than anything else. It flows continuously, independent of your opinions, your expectations, or the countless hours you spend analyzing charts late into the night.

Before you wake up in the morning, the flow is already there. Long after you fall asleep, it continues moving forward. And even when traders eventually disappear from the market — exhausted, discouraged, or broken after losing everything they had — the flow remains exactly as it always has: indifferent, endless, and untouched by any individual participant.

The river does not hate you, nor does it favor you. It simply flows according to its own nature. And within that flow, you are merely a leaf drifting through the current.

At first, that may sound small, perhaps even a little helpless. But it is worth thinking about more carefully before reaching that conclusion. A leaf drifting on the water is neither useless nor completely powerless. It cannot control the current itself, but it can still position itself within that current. When it aligns with the main flow, it can travel surprisingly far. When it resists the direction of the water, it is eventually pulled under. If it drifts too close to the edge, it slowly decays over time. And if it becomes trapped inside a whirlpool, it may continue spinning endlessly without ever truly going anywhere. The difference has nothing to do with which branch the leaf came from, whether it is large or small, fragile or resilient. In the end, everything depends on one thing alone: whether it is positioned in harmony with the flow of the river.

That is the true essence of trading. Not prediction. Not control. And certainly not conquest. It is positioning.

For many years, one question has been repeated over and over throughout the trading world: Why do most people lose? Countless explanations have been offered. Lack of knowledge. Lack of discipline. Lack of capital. Lack of experience. All of those answers contain some truth, yet they all overlook something far more fundamental.

Most traders lose because they fail to understand that they are standing inside a river.

They enter the market with the mindset of a conqueror. They believe they can analyze, predict, and force profits out of the market through sheer intelligence or effort. They draw trendlines on charts as though they are mapping fixed territory, without realizing that a river has no permanent map. Its shape changes after every storm. They study the news and assume they understand where the market is headed, failing to recognize that news events are often nothing more than ripples on the surface, while the true current beneath has already been shaped by forces far larger than themselves.

And when the current finally pulls them away, they blame themselves for miscalculating. Or they blame the market for being irrational. Or they blame the mentors and systems they once trusted. Very few ever stop long enough to ask the more important question: Do I truly understand the nature of the river I am trying to navigate?

This book is not built around the idea of predicting the market. If you are looking for a perfect formula, a hidden indicator, or a strategy capable of producing guaranteed profits, you will not find it in these pages — not because anyone is withholding the answer from you, but because no such answer truly exists.

The real purpose of this book is far simpler and far more important: to change the way you perceive the market itself. Before a trader can perform consistently, they must first learn to see the market correctly. Most traders do not lose simply because they make poor decisions. They lose because the picture they carry in their minds is fundamentally different from the reality unfolding on the chart in front of them.

The market is not a small stream that can be understood from the surface alone. It is a deep and constantly shifting river shaped by forces far beyond what most retail traders can observe directly. Beneath every visible movement lies another layer of flow — institutional capital moving across markets, central bank policies influencing liquidity, algorithms reacting within milliseconds — all quietly guiding price in ways that are often impossible to recognize at first glance.

Fortunately, a leaf drifting on the river does not need to understand the entire system. It only needs to feel the current where it is. From there, the decision becomes surprisingly simple: move with the flow or fight against it. In many respects, trading is not much more complicated than that.

The goal is to become a wiser leaf.

Not the kind that stubbornly fights the flow until it is eventually crushed by it. And not the kind that drifts aimlessly without awareness, only to end up trapped in stagnant water. A good leaf learns to listen to the current. It senses the direction of the flow before the force of the river fully takes hold, and it positions itself carefully enough for the water to become an ally rather than an enemy.

Fibonacci and the Endless Battle

When traders draw a Fibonacci grid on a chart, they are not uncovering some hidden prediction tool. They are simply identifying price zones where the market may become more responsive than usual. The 0.618 level. The 0.5 level. The 0.382 level. These levels function more like reference points along a river, highlighting areas where the flow of price may begin to slow down, hesitate, or change direction.

But the reference point itself does not determine what the market will do next.

This is one of the earliest misconceptions many traders develop when learning Fibonacci. They see price reach the 0.618 level and immediately execute a trade, as though the level itself automatically creates a buying or selling opportunity.

A Fibonacci level is always projected before price arrives there. You measure a completed move, project the retracement levels forward, and wait for the market to revisit those areas in the future. But at that moment, the future remains uncertain territory. The market has not revealed its intentions yet. No real decision has been made. Until price actually reaches the zone and begins interacting with it, every expectation remains theoretical.

So once price finally reaches a Fibonacci zone, what do you actually need next? You need something Fibonacci alone can never provide: confirmation. You need the market itself to reveal what is happening inside that area. And the most direct, immediate, and honest source of that information is the ongoing battle between Bulls and Bears.

At first glance, this idea may sound old-fashioned, even simplistic. Most traders are introduced to the concepts of Bulls and Bears during their earliest days in the market. Rising prices represent bullish conditions. Falling prices represent bearish conditions. For many people, the terms become nothing more than labels describing market direction, simple metaphors with little depth beyond that.

But that interpretation misses the point entirely.

Bulls and Bears are not merely descriptions of price movement. They represent opposing forces competing for control over every price zone, every candlestick, and every moment that unfolds in the market. That struggle never disappears. It never becomes outdated simply because new indicators or more sophisticated trading tools are introduced. In reality, every technical tool — every indicator, candlestick pattern, or market structure model — is ultimately just another way of observing and measuring this underlying conflict from a different perspective.

So how does this battle actually unfold?

Each side fights using two things: **force** and **territory**.

Force determines the strength behind an attack, and in the market, that strength is reflected through the character and momentum of price movement itself. When price rises with strong momentum — sharp, decisive, and continuous — it signals aggressive buying pressure from the Bulls. But when price climbs slowly, hesitates constantly, and struggles to maintain direction, the advance may still be moving upward while lacking real strength underneath.

A weak attack can push price forward temporarily, but that alone does not guarantee control over the territory that was gained. Once the opposing side launches a counterattack, fragile momentum often collapses quickly. A strong attack, however, leaves a visible mark on the chart. It creates conviction. And the price zone where that movement began often becomes meaningful territory defended by the side that originally seized it.

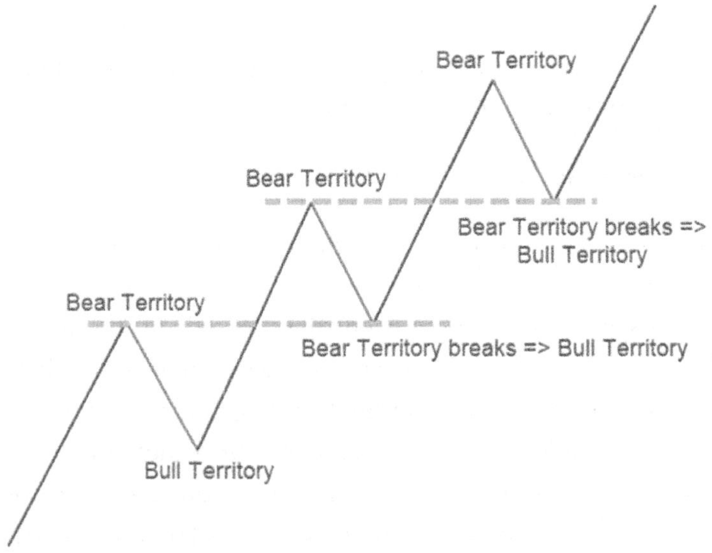

Figure 1.1: Bull and Bear Territories

Territory is where each side gathers strength, reinforces its position, and prepares for the next phase of battle. On a chart, Bull territory consists of areas where price previously rallied with clear buying pressure — zones where buyers successfully defended the market in the past and may be willing to step in again if price returns. Bear territory works the same way in the opposite direction. These are areas where sellers previously forced price lower and left behind evidence of strong selling interest.

If the Bulls generate enough strength to break through and establish acceptance above the Bears' former territory, control begins to shift. Old resistance turns into new support. But if the Bears successfully defend the zone, price is pushed back once again, and the conflict continues inside a range until one side eventually builds enough pressure to break the balance decisively (Figure 1.1).

There are also periods when this struggle unfolds within a narrower price range.

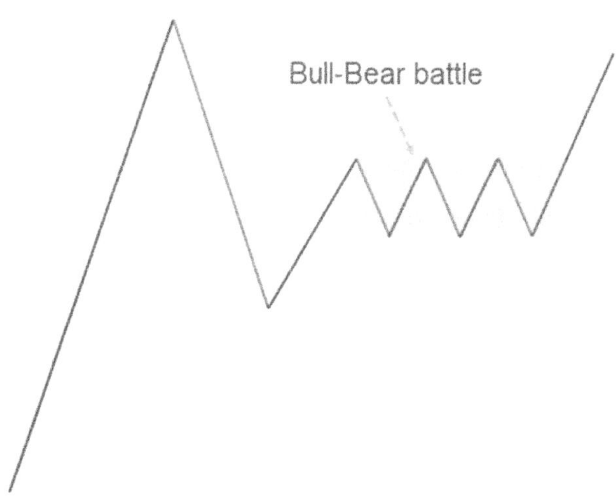

Figure 1.2: Bull-Bear Battle in a Narrow Range

At times, the market behaves very differently from the clean and decisive swings traders are used to seeing. Instead of sharp advances followed by equally aggressive counterattacks, the battle becomes quieter and far less obvious on the surface. Price appears to go nowhere. It lingers within a narrow range, drifting back and forth without producing any meaningful breakout.

This does not necessarily mean the market is weak. More often, it means the struggle between Bulls and Bears has reached a temporary balance. Both sides are actively fighting for control inside that area, yet neither possesses enough strength to end the battle decisively.

Figure 1.3: Bull-Bear battle in a narrow range

If you study Figure 1.3 carefully, you will notice that price seems repeatedly drawn back into the same area. It touches the zone, reacts briefly, then returns again. The cycle repeats over and over. Candles become messy and directionless. Small candle bodies begin to appear alongside long wicks sweeping both sides of the range — clear signs of intense conflict without a decisive winner. This is what happens when Bull and Bear territory sit extremely close to one another, with both sides constantly testing the limits of the other without yet possessing enough strength to force a true breakout.

Many traders ignore this type of price action because it appears as though "nothing is happening." In reality, this is often where the market is making some of its most important decisions. Energy is building beneath the surface. Pressure is accumulating. Eventually, one side begins to weaken, and once that happens, the opposing side is usually able to break away with remarkable force. The energy spent during the prolonged struggle is suddenly released all at once. This is why breakouts emerging from compression and consolidation phases often appear far sharper and more decisive than breakouts formed during smooth trending conditions.

When this kind of compression develops around an important Fibonacci level — or when the structure is supported by momentum from a nearby Fibonacci zone — the situation becomes significantly more meaningful. The Fibonacci level itself highlights the area as important, while the price action confirms that both buyers and sellers also recognize its importance strongly enough to fight over it. Do not dismiss these situations simply because there is not yet a perfect-looking entry candle. At times, the market's hesitation communicates far more than immediate movement ever could.

Now let us return to Fibonacci.

You have drawn the retracement grid. Price is approaching the 0.618 zone, and like every trader using Fibonacci, you are waiting for the market to reveal its next move. But the important question is not whether the level itself will hold. The real question is far more meaningful: once price reaches that area, which side is beginning to gain control of the battle?

What matters is the behavior unfolding around it. How strong is the selling pressure as price moves into the zone? Is the decline sharp and aggressive enough to suggest that the Bears remain firmly in control? Or is momentum beginning to weaken? Once price reaches the Fibonacci area, do buyers respond with conviction and reclaim territory, or does the market hesitate briefly before continuing lower as though the level barely existed at all? Has this zone previously acted as an area where Bulls successfully defended price in the past?

These are the questions that actually matter.

The market never moves without an underlying reason. Every breakout above resistance represents a moment when buyers finally accumulate enough strength to overpower sellers defending that territory. Every reversal from support reflects the opposite process — selling pressure gradually weakening while buyers regain control. Trends, pullbacks, consolidations, and explosive expansions are all visible expressions of the same invisible conflict unfolding beneath price.

Once you begin to understand the market through that lens, charts stop looking like collections of random candlesticks. Instead, they begin to resemble a living battlefield. You start recognizing who is attacking, who is defending, which areas are being contested, and where control is slowly shifting from one side to the other. The flow of the river becomes easier to feel. And once you can feel that flow, positioning yourself within the market becomes very different from trying to predict where it will go next.

CHAPTER 2: BEFORE THE SETUP

Fibonacci is a powerful tool, but like any tool in trading, its effectiveness depends entirely on when, where, and how it is applied. This chapter is not about how to draw Fibonacci levels. It is about something far more important: understanding when Fibonacci should be used, when it should be avoided, and when market conditions are genuinely aligned in your favor.

Most of the frustration traders experience with Fibonacci does not come from drawing the levels incorrectly. More often, the problem lies in applying the tool within the wrong context. Traders use a trend-based measurement tool in markets that lack directional structure, or they react to a visually appealing setup while ignoring the more important question beneath it: is the market actually ready to move?

This chapter explores those questions in a structured and practical way. We will examine the types of market conditions where Fibonacci tends to lose reliability, as well as the factors that cause certain Fibonacci zones to become significantly more meaningful than others. Everything that follows later in this book is built upon this foundation.

Sideways Market

One of the most common habits traders develop when using Fibonacci — often from their very first days in the market — is the tendency to draw far too many retracement grids. Every swing suddenly feels important enough to measure. A minor rally, a brief pullback, or even a random intraday fluctuation quickly becomes another set of 0.382, 0.5, and 0.618 levels projected across the chart. At first, this creates the impression of detailed analysis. It feels as though the trader is studying the market carefully and leaving no movement unnoticed. But the more grids that appear on the chart, the more crowded everything becomes. Horizontal levels begin overlapping one another until nearly every price zone starts looking significant.

That is usually when the real problem begins. Once everything resembles a signal, nothing truly functions as one anymore.

Traders start seeing opportunities everywhere. Price touches a small Fibonacci level and they immediately anticipate a reversal. A few reactive candles appear and suddenly they believe a new trend is beginning. Trades become more frequent, decisions become more impulsive, and attention shifts toward every minor fluctuation in price. Over time, many traders become trapped in something even more dangerous than losing trades themselves: market noise.

One important reality is often ignored throughout this process. Most markets spend the majority of their time without a clear directional trend. During many periods, price simply oscillates back and forth within relatively narrow ranges — rising, falling, then rising again without creating meaningful continuation in either direction. These movements produce countless small swings that appear important when viewed individually, yet ultimately lead nowhere. The chart remains active and visually busy, but beneath that activity, there is very little genuine flow driving the market forward.

Fibonacci performs best when the market is genuinely moving — when there is a clear trend, visible momentum, and a meaningful imbalance between Bulls and Bears strong enough to produce a significant price swing. But in noisy market conditions, where price simply fluctuates without direction, drawing Fibonacci levels across every small movement becomes little more than an attempt to find structure inside randomness. The levels still appear on the chart. Minor reactions still occur around them. But most of those reactions carry very little real significance.

To understand Fibonacci properly, it is necessary to return to its original purpose. Fibonacci is primarily used to measure the depth of a pullback within an existing trend. Its entire logic depends on one core assumption: after a strong directional move, the market will temporarily retrace part of that movement before continuing in the original direction. Fibonacci levels simply identify the areas where that retracement may end and where the dominant trend may begin to assert itself again.

But that logic only works when a genuine trend already exists.

If the market has no clear direction, then there is effectively nothing meaningful to measure. In sideways conditions, there is no dominant flow driving price forward. Instead, the market becomes a constant struggle between buyers and sellers inside a relatively narrow range, where rallies are repeatedly sold and declines are repeatedly bought. Neither side gains lasting control. Under those conditions, a small price swing does not represent a true trend; it merely reflects another fluctuation inside the noise.

And when Fibonacci is applied to noise, the levels themselves become unreliable. They may still produce random reactions, but those reactions lack structural meaning because they are not connected to a larger directional flow. Fibonacci requires trend structure in the same way a river requires a current. Applying Fibonacci inside a directionless market is like placing a leaf onto stagnant water and expecting it to drift downstream. Without a current, the leaf goes nowhere.

Therefore, before even thinking about drawing Fibonacci, the most important step is not choosing the high or the low, but filtering out noise. The first question to answer is not "Where should I draw the Fibonacci?" but "Is the market actually trending right now?" If the answer is no — if price is simply fluctuating within a narrow range, if buyers and sellers are still locked in equilibrium with neither side gaining clear control — then the correct action is not to look for opportunities, but to do nothing. No drawing, no measuring, no trading — just waiting.

This is what most traders struggle to do, not because they do not understand it, but because watching the market without taking action creates the feeling of missing out on opportunities. Once price starts moving, the brain automatically interprets that movement as opportunity, and the urge to draw the Fibonacci grid begins from there. But in trading, doing nothing when conditions are not aligned is not missing an opportunity — it is a trading decision in itself. Preserving capital during long periods of noise so that you are ready for genuine trending conditions is a strategy, not passivity.

When the Price Bounces Too Quickly from Fibonacci Levels

There is a particular situation that almost every long-term Fibonacci trader eventually experiences, and it tends to create a uniquely frustrating feeling. The loss itself is often not catastrophic. The analysis is not entirely wrong either. In fact, the trade can feel painfully close to being correct, which is exactly what makes the experience so difficult. It feels as though you followed the textbook properly, yet the market still found a way to punish you.

The scenario usually unfolds in a familiar way.

The market is clearly trending upward. Price has already produced a strong bullish swing before beginning a pullback. You draw your Fibonacci grid, identify the key retracement zones, and wait patiently for price to reach them. Eventually, the market retraces into the 0.5 level — an area you had already marked in advance. Then, almost immediately, a reversal candle appears. The candle looks convincing: a strong bullish close, a clean rejection from the level, and enough momentum to suggest that buyers may be stepping back into the market. Everything appears technically correct. So you enter a long position.

At first, the trade even seems to work. Price pushes upward for a short period, hesitates briefly, then suddenly reverses lower again. The

Fibonacci level you trusted breaks apart, price drops deeper than expected, and your stop-loss is eventually hit before the market finally finds support and resumes the original uptrend.

And that is what makes this situation so psychologically frustrating. Your broader market idea was not actually wrong. The trend did continue upward in the end. The problem was simply that the correction had not finished yet. The market needed a deeper retracement before buyers were truly ready to regain control.

So what actually happened in that situation?

The answer was not hidden inside the Fibonacci level itself, nor inside the reversal candle that appeared at the zone. The real issue was something far more subtle: the market never went through a genuine period of conflict.

When price reaches a Fibonacci level and immediately bounces away from it, the struggle between Bulls and Bears is often still incomplete. There is no real hesitation, no compression, no visible phase where both sides actively test one another before one side gradually weakens and the other begins taking control. Price simply touches the level and reacts instantly, almost like a ball bouncing off the floor without any meaningful fight taking place around it.

And that creates an important problem. A reaction without conflict tells us little about the true strength behind the move. In many cases, when price reaches a Fibonacci zone too quickly and reverses too quickly, the opposing side — in this case, the Bears — has not actually been defeated yet. They simply have not fully entered the battle. Selling pressure has not been exhausted, and the market has not gone through the process of forcing one side to surrender territory. A side that has not truly lost control can easily return later with stronger participation and enough momentum to continue pushing price in its original direction.

What makes this situation dangerous is that, on the surface, everything looks almost perfect. A clean reversal candle forming precisely at a Fibonacci level is exactly the type of setup Fibonacci traders are taught to look for. The location appears correct. The candlestick pattern appears convincing. The broader trend still aligns with the trade. From a psychological perspective, the chart seems filled with confirmation.

But a beautiful candle cannot replace a completed process.

No matter how impressive a reversal pattern looks, it only reflects what happened during one or several candles. It says very little about whether the market has actually resolved the underlying battle taking place at that zone. A strong pin bar rejecting the 0.5 retracement level may simply represent a temporary technical bounce before sellers regroup and continue driving price deeper into the correction.

This is why the consolidation and hesitation discussed earlier matter so much. In this context, they are not merely interesting patterns; they function as a filter. They provide evidence that both sides truly participated in the battle, that buyers and sellers actively fought for control of the zone, and that one side gradually weakened before the other finally gained dominance. Without that process, there is very little real confirmation behind the setup. There is only a clean-looking candle sitting on top of a Fibonacci number, and by itself, that is rarely enough.

Of course, this approach comes with a trade-off. There will absolutely be times when price reaches a Fibonacci level and reverses immediately without any meaningful consolidation at all. The market moves sharply, the trend resumes, and the opportunity disappears without you participating in it. This is not uncommon. Any trader who stays in the market long enough will encounter these situations repeatedly. But the important question is not whether you will occasionally miss fast reversals. The real question is whether that patience and caution improve your long-term decision-making overall.

In my experience, the answer is yes. Every time you avoid chasing an immediate reversal without proper confirmation, you are also protecting yourself from the many situations where the setup initially appears perfect, only for price to continue pushing deeper into the retracement — toward levels such as 0.786 — before eventually stopping out traders who entered too early.

Zones or Exact Levels?

I discussed this idea briefly in *Secrets on Fibonacci Trading*, but it deserves far more emphasis here because of how important it becomes in real trading conditions. In fact, nearly every example throughout this book will be built around Fibonacci zones rather than precise individual levels.

One of the most common mistakes traders make with Fibonacci retracements is becoming overly fixated on exact numbers. They wait specifically for the 0.618 retracement. Or the 0.5 level. Or the 0.382 level. The mindset sounds disciplined on the surface, but in practice it often causes traders to miss high-quality opportunities simply because price reacted inside a Fibonacci zone instead of touching the precise level they had in mind.

The market does not operate with mathematical precision. Price is under no obligation to touch an exact number before reversing. In reality, markets behave far more fluidly than that. Most of the time, price fluctuates within an area — often between two neighboring Fibonacci levels — while buyers and sellers continue testing one another before the next directional move begins to emerge.

The space between the 0.5 and 0.618 retracement levels is a perfect example. Price may spend time oscillating within that region, probing liquidity, testing conviction from both sides, and gradually revealing where control is shifting. If a trader stubbornly waits for price to reach the exact 0.618 level before paying attention, there is a good chance the meaningful signal has already appeared — and perhaps even completed — before that level is ever touched.

When Price Stops at an Exact Fibonacci Level

There are certainly situations where price retraces and reacts almost perfectly at a specific Fibonacci level — especially around the 0.618 retracement. When that happens, the reaction deserves attention. That level of precision often suggests that the market is responding very sensitively to a particular support or resistance area. But it is important to understand what this actually represents. It is an ideal scenario, not a mandatory requirement.

Treating perfect precision as the only acceptable condition for taking a trade unnecessarily limits the number of valid opportunities available in the market. In practice, price rarely behaves with that level of mathematical cleanliness on a consistent basis. Traders who become obsessed with exact Fibonacci touches often end up ignoring strong setups that develop naturally within broader Fibonacci zones simply because the market stopped a few points short of the number they were waiting for.

Zones Create a Balance Between Precision and Flexibility

The real advantage of trading Fibonacci as zones rather than exact levels is that it creates enough room for the market to reveal meaningful behavior without forcing the trader into making decisions at a single precise price point. Instead of asking, "Has price touched the exact 0.618 level yet?" the more useful question becomes, "Has price entered an important area, and if so, how is the market behaving inside that area?"

That shift in perspective changes everything.

The second question provides far more information because it keeps the trader engaged with price action itself rather than passively waiting for a specific number to be reached. It encourages observation instead of prediction. More importantly, it reflects the way markets actually move in real conditions.

At its core, Fibonacci retracement should not be viewed as a collection of exact points on a chart. It is better understood as a framework of pressure zones — areas where reactions become more likely and where the balance between buyers and sellers may begin to shift. Once traders start seeing Fibonacci through that lens, the entire way they apply the tool begins to change naturally.

When Multiple Forces Converge

As mentioned earlier, Fibonacci does not operate in isolation. A Fibonacci level or retracement zone becomes meaningful not because the number itself possesses any special power, but because other market factors begin converging around the same area. The more independent forces pointing toward a single price zone, the greater the probability that the market will respond meaningfully there.

In this section, we will examine three of the strongest forms of confluence when trading with Fibonacci: the alignment between Fibonacci zones and major support or resistance levels, the role of multi-timeframe analysis, and the importance of the Golden Fibonacci retracement zone between 0.5 and 0.618.

When Fibonacci Meets Support and Resistance

In real trading conditions, many high-probability setups emerge when a Fibonacci retracement zone aligns with an important support or resistance level that has already been validated by the market. This type of confluence is not random. It reflects something much more meaningful: two independent analytical frameworks are identifying the same area as important, which naturally increases the significance of that zone in the eyes of both buyers and sellers.

One of the clearest examples appears after price successfully breaks above a major swing high. As discussed earlier, once a resistance level is convincingly broken, it often begins acting as support when price later revisits the area. A zone that was previously defended by the Bears gradually transforms into territory the Bulls are willing to protect. When a pullback eventually brings price back into that former resistance area — and the same zone also aligns with an important Fibonacci retracement level or retracement zone — the market enters a powerful confluence environment.

At that point, two different perspectives are reinforcing the same idea simultaneously. Market structure suggests that buyers may defend the previous breakout area, while Fibonacci identifies the same region as a potential retracement completion zone. When both forms of analysis point toward the same location, the probability of a meaningful reaction increases significantly (Figure 2.1).

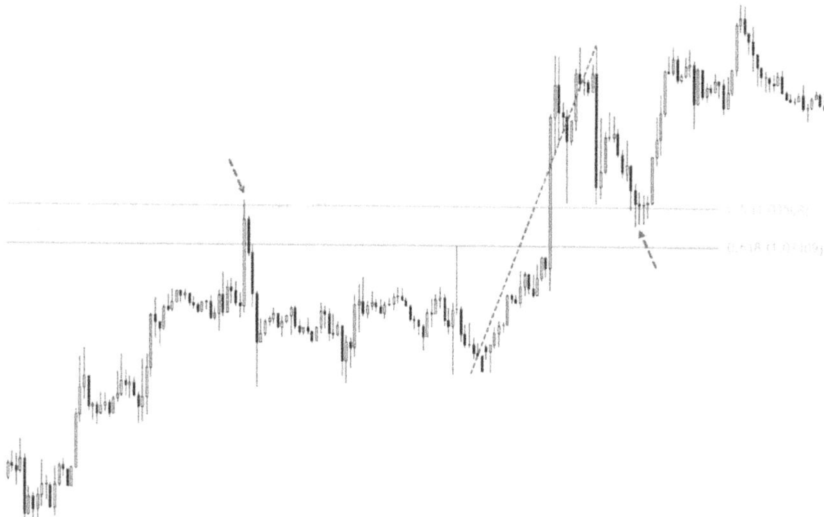

Figure 2.1: Fibonacci Confluence

Figure 2.1 illustrates a situation where a previous resistance level aligns directly with the 0.5–0.618 Fibonacci retracement zone. What makes this type of setup especially powerful is that the logic supporting it exists from both perspectives simultaneously. From a Fibonacci standpoint, the 0.5–0.618 zone represents a healthy and natural retracement within a strong trend — deep enough to absorb selling pressure, but not deep enough to invalidate the broader bullish structure. From a support and resistance perspective, the former swing high that has just been broken is already an important market area. It is a zone where large amounts of trading activity previously occurred, where buyers and sellers actively fought for control, and where price reactions therefore tend to carry greater significance.

Of course, support and resistance do not originate solely from broken highs and lows. Important levels can also emerge from prolonged accumulation ranges, major consolidation structures, or clear supply and demand zones visible on higher timeframes. But the underlying principle remains the same. Whenever one of these structural areas aligns with a Fibonacci retracement zone already under observation, the confluence strengthens the setup and provides another reason to pay closer attention to the price behavior developing there.

Multi-Timeframe Observation

Another important tool you will see repeatedly throughout this book is multi-timeframe analysis. Even when a trader fully understands a strategy, becoming too focused on a single timeframe can still lead to missed opportunities or force entries with unnecessarily poor quality.

Lower timeframes often reveal what is hidden inside the candles of a higher timeframe. A sequence of mixed bullish and bearish candles on a 4-hour chart may appear unclear at first glance, yet the same price action can reveal a complete consolidation structure with well-defined highs and lows on the 1-hour chart. The battle between buyers and sellers becomes easier to follow because the underlying struggle is displayed in greater detail.

And in many situations, simply stepping down to a lower timeframe can uncover a cleaner price structure where stop-loss placement becomes tighter, more logical, and more efficient. Instead of using a wide stop based entirely on the higher timeframe structure — which often weakens the reward-to-risk profile unnecessarily — the lower timeframe may provide a more precise area where the market has already revealed meaningful support or resistance.

This is not the kind of skill that can be memorized mechanically. It develops gradually through observation and screen time. As you move through the examples in this book, you will begin noticing how different timeframes complement one another, until switching between them becomes a natural part of reading market structure itself.

Fibonacci Golden Zone - 0.5 — 0.618

When these elements come together, the 0.5–0.618 Fibonacci retracement zone becomes far more than a mathematical range on a chart. It becomes an area where market structure, trader psychology, and price behavior begin converging in meaningful ways.

So why does this area attract so much attention among traders?

The first reason lies in its positioning within the retracement itself. Entering around the 0.5–0.618 zone means price has already corrected deeply enough to create genuine tension in the market, but not so deeply that the broader trend structure begins falling apart. The pullback is large enough for the opposing side to participate meaningfully and reveal its strength, yet still shallow enough for the dominant trend to remain structurally healthy. In many cases, this creates the ideal environment for price action analysis because the market has enough room to develop real conflict, form natural confirmation signals, and establish logical areas for stop-loss placement.

More importantly, trades initiated around the 0.5–0.618 zone often maintain sufficient room for price to travel toward the most natural profit target available: the 0% level, which represents the previous swing high where the earlier bullish movement originally stalled and began retracing. This is not an arbitrary take-profit target. The prior high is a meaningful area because it marks the point where sellers previously entered the market with enough strength to interrupt the trend. In other words, it remains an important piece of Bear territory, which means selling pressure may reappear once price revisits the area.

In practical terms, the distance between the Golden Zone and the prior swing high also tends to produce attractive reward-to-risk conditions in many setups. The market does not need to generate an unusually large move to justify the trade. It simply needs to resume the existing trend in a relatively normal and healthy manner.

In the next two chapters, we will focus specifically on trading strategies that develop after price enters the 0.5–0.618 Golden Zone — a retracement region that appears frequently across many different market environments, whether the market is preparing for a reversal or continuing within a strong trending phase.

When you step back and look at everything covered in this chapter, one central idea connects all of it: Fibonacci does not function in isolation. It requires context. It requires the right conditions. And more importantly, it requires the trader using it to recognize the difference between a market that is genuinely supporting a setup and a market that is merely creating the illusion of opportunity.

A sideways market is not the enemy; it is simply an environment where Fibonacci loses much of its effectiveness. A sharp reaction from a Fibonacci level is not necessarily a bad signal; it is often just an incomplete one. And a Fibonacci zone by itself is not meaningless, but its importance increases dramatically when additional forces begin converging around the same area.

Trading Fibonacci through zones rather than exact levels, paying attention to support and resistance confluence, aligning analysis across multiple timeframes, and understanding the special significance of the 0.5–0.618 Golden Zone — none of these ideas should be treated as rigid rules that must be followed mechanically. They are better understood as lenses that help traders see market behavior more clearly and make decisions based on stronger underlying logic rather than isolated signals.

In the next chapter, we will begin applying these foundations in real trading situations, where the focus shifts toward reading the battle between Bulls and Bears in order to identify high-quality entry opportunities.

CHAPTER 3: EQUILIBRIUM BREAKOUT STRATEGY

In trading, not every retracement carries the same meaning. Some pullbacks remain shallow, giving the opposing side very little opportunity to fight back before the trend resumes. Others unfold more slowly and retrace much deeper, creating the impression that the market is hesitating or reconsidering its direction before making the next meaningful move.

Many traders interpret deep retracements as signs of trend weakness. In reality, however, they often represent something very different: a necessary rebalancing process before the market continues moving in the original direction. That idea forms the foundation of the Equilibrium Breakout strategy.

Throughout this chapter, we will focus on situations where price retraces into the 0.5–0.618 Fibonacci zone before continuing with the dominant trend. This area often represents a temporary equilibrium within the broader price swing — a phase where buyers begin returning to absorb selling pressure while sellers simultaneously attempt to defend their remaining positions. It is essentially a redistribution of control between Bulls and Bears before the market fully commits to its next move.

For that reason, the goal is not to enter immediately simply because price touches the Fibonacci zone. Instead, we wait patiently and observe how the market behaves inside the area. We are not looking for a random bounce. We are looking for evidence of conflict, evidence that one side is gradually exhausting itself, and most importantly, evidence of a breakout strong enough to show that control has genuinely shifted in favor of one side.

In the next section, we will explore the anatomy of breakout behavior itself, including the difference between a simple price break and a breakout that carries genuine structural weight.

The Art of Breakouts: Why a Single High Is Not Enough

In technical analysis, the concept of a breakout is often reduced to a simple idea: price moves above a previous high. But for a sustainable advanced Fibonacci strategy, a breakout must be understood as something far more meaningful than a single event on a chart. A true breakout is the visible result of a deeper transfer of control between Bulls and Bears.

From a structural perspective, a swing high represents an area where sellers previously defended their territory successfully and prevented buyers from pushing the market higher. When price eventually breaks through that area, it signals that the Bears are no longer able to maintain control and that buying pressure has begun overpowering the defense. But for serious traders, the important question is not whether price broke resistance. The real question is what kind of breakout is actually capable of producing high-probability continuation afterward.

The answer lies in the structure of the resistance itself.

In real market conditions, a breakout above a single isolated high often carries hidden risks. One rejected high simply tells us that sellers defended the market successfully once. It does not necessarily mean their selling pressure has been exhausted. In many cases, sellers are merely stepping back temporarily before attempting to defend the market again from a higher area.

A breakout with real structural weight usually develops differently. It tends to emerge only after price has repeatedly attacked the same resistance zone multiple times or after the market has spent time consolidating beneath the area through prolonged sideways compression. Under those conditions, the market begins revealing something important: sellers are being forced to absorb repeated buying pressure while gradually losing the ability to push price meaningfully lower. The battle is no longer a single rejection. It becomes a process of exhaustion.

The Psychology Behind Multi-Top Resistance Zones

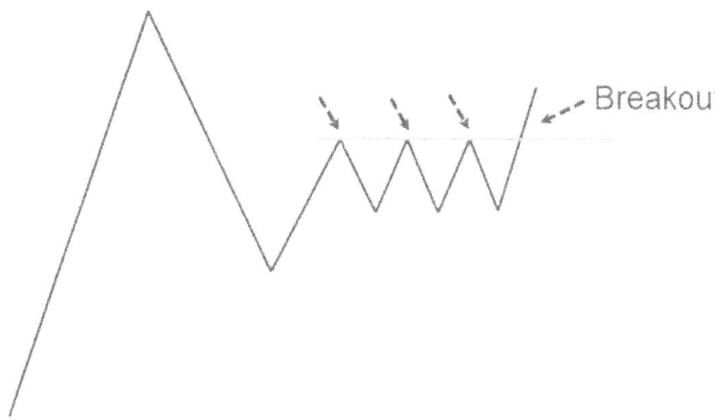

Figure 3.1: Ideal breakout scenario

Imagine the market as a battlefield between two opposing armies: Bulls and Bears. If the Bears control a force of 10,000 soldiers but only commit 1,000 of them to defend the first major high, they still retain enormous reserves capable of creating additional selling pressure later. This is one reason why breakouts above a single isolated high often struggle to produce strong continuation. The selling side may have defended only lightly, meaning a large amount of supply still remains available above the market.

The situation changes when price repeatedly tests the same resistance zone and forms multiple highs around the same area. Each time the market pushes into resistance and gets rejected, the Bears are forced to commit additional resources to maintain control. In trading terms, that means more sell orders, more liquidity consumption, and more effort spent defending the same territory. The repeated defense itself becomes meaningful because it reveals that sellers view the area as strategically important.

Eventually, if price continues attacking the zone without producing significant downward follow-through, the balance of power begins shifting beneath the surface. Sellers are gradually forced to absorb wave after wave of buying pressure while becoming less effective at pushing the market lower. By the time the resistance finally breaks, the breakout carries a much stronger message: the Bears have already spent a substantial portion of their defensive strength and still failed to hold the line.

That is why breakouts above multi-top resistance zones often behave very differently from breakouts above a single isolated high. Once the defense collapses after repeated testing, the market frequently encounters far less resistance overhead, allowing price to accelerate more aggressively and travel farther in a relatively short period of time.

Price Compression: The Key to Explosive Breakouts

Beyond the presence of multiple highs, an ideal breakout structure is often accompanied by a period of hesitation and tight consolidation near the resistance zone itself. In advanced price action analysis, this behavior is commonly referred to as price compression.

In nature, many things produce their greatest force only after being compressed for a sufficient period of time. A tightly compressed spring releases with greater energy. A bow pulled farther back launches the arrow with greater speed. Even a twisted rubber band stores tension before snapping back violently. Markets behave in much the same way. Periods that appear slow, indecisive, or lacking momentum are often the exact moments when energy is quietly building beneath the surface for the next major expansion.

Compression develops when price no longer reacts to resistance with deep pullbacks. Instead, each decline becomes shallower than the previous one. Higher lows begin forming while the highs remain relatively fixed, gradually squeezing price into an increasingly narrow range beneath resistance. Structurally, this behavior reveals something important: buyers are continuing to absorb supply and apply upward pressure without allowing the market to retrace deeply. The Bears are still defending the area, but their ability to force meaningful downside movement is beginning to weaken.

Once the compression reaches its limit and price finally breaks out of the structure, the move often resembles a compressed spring suddenly being released. Momentum expands rapidly because the market has already spent considerable time building pressure beneath the surface before the breakout itself occurred.

When this type of compression develops around a Fibonacci retracement zone, the structure becomes even more valuable. The compression not only confirms persistent buying pressure, but also creates a very logical and efficient area for stop-loss placement beneath the most recent structural lows inside the compressed range. From a trade management perspective, this dramatically improves the reward-to-risk profile of the setup, allowing traders to pursue meaningful opportunities without requiring price to travel unusually far in order to produce attractive returns.

In the next section, we will begin integrating Fibonacci directly into this framework in order to identify the most efficient retracement zones after the breakout itself — areas where the market not only offers trend continuation opportunities, but does so at prices that allow for far more favorable positioning and reward-to-risk conditions.

Equilibrium Breakout Strategy

To make the strategy easier to understand and apply consistently, I have distilled the entire process into four core steps. The framework combines higher-level structural analysis with the precise moments where short-term momentum begins expanding into a larger directional move.

Step 1: Identify the Market Context and Fibonacci Zone

Begin by analyzing the broader price structure to confirm the presence of an uptrend, typically identified by price successfully breaking above a previous significant high. Once the market forms a new swing high and begins retracing, apply the Fibonacci Retracement tool to the completed bullish swing and focus primarily on the 0.5–0.618 Golden Zone. This area represents a natural equilibrium within the trend structure. In many cases, this is where buyers begin gradually rebuilding positions in preparation for a potential continuation of the upward move.

Step 2: Wait for a Period of Conflict and Compression

Figure 3.1: Breakout patterns

Once price retraces into the 0.5–0.618 Fibonacci zone, the next step is to observe the interaction between Bulls and Bears carefully. This is the phase where the market reveals whether the retracement is merely a temporary pause within the trend or the beginning of something deeper. The key is not the Fibonacci level itself, but the struggle unfolding around it.

These periods of conflict gradually force one side to expend energy, creating the conditions for the opposing side to regain control. Depending on the market environment, this process can be analyzed directly on the current timeframe or examined more closely through a lower timeframe structure. Figure 3.1 illustrates two common variations of this behavior.

The structure on the left represents a period of conflict without clear price compression. Bulls and Bears repeatedly fight within a relatively stable range, producing highs and lows that remain roughly horizontal. After enough back-and-forth movement inside the range, a breakout beyond the structure often provides a solid continuation signal.

The structure on the right is less common, but generally stronger. In this case, the conflict develops alongside visible price compression. The highs remain relatively equal while the lows gradually rise higher and higher, creating a tightening structure that can be recognized visually without difficulty. This behavior reflects increasing buying pressure beneath the surface while sellers become progressively less capable of forcing meaningful pullbacks. By the time a breakout finally occurs, the market often transitions rapidly from consolidation into expansion as buyers overwhelm the remaining resistance.

Step 3: Entry and Stop-Loss Placement

We only take action once the market produces a decisive breakout candle through the multi-top resistance structure. Ideally, the breakout candle should display strong momentum with a clear and extended body, while avoiding long upper wicks that suggest immediate rejection from the breakout area.

- Entry: Enter the trade once the breakout candle closes convincingly above the structure.
- Stop-Loss (SL): Place the stop-loss beneath the nearest structural low within the compression pattern.

Step 4: Take-profit placement

When it comes to take-profit management, the highest priority should always be consistency, discipline, and capital protection. Depending on the broader market context, one approach is to secure partial profits at the 0% Fibonacci level — the previous swing high — while leaving the remaining portion of the position open for higher key levels farther ahead. In other situations, closing the entire trade may be the more appropriate decision once the reward achieved is already satisfactory, typically around 2R or higher.

Trade management is too important to treat as a minor detail within the strategy itself. For that reason, a separate chapter later in the book will focus entirely on take-profit logic, position management, and the decision-making process behind protecting gains while still allowing strong trades enough room to develop.

Trade Example 1

To bring the breakout concepts discussed earlier into a real trading context, let us examine a practical market scenario where structured price behavior, Fibonacci retracement logic, and breakout dynamics align to create a high-probability setup.

The process is less about predicting the market and more about preparing for a specific situation in advance. In many ways, it resembles setting a carefully designed trap. The structure, the Fibonacci zone, and the conditions for confirmation are all identified beforehand. Once the framework is in place, the objective is no longer to chase the market impulsively, but to remain patient and wait for price to move naturally into the area where the opportunity has the highest probability of developing.

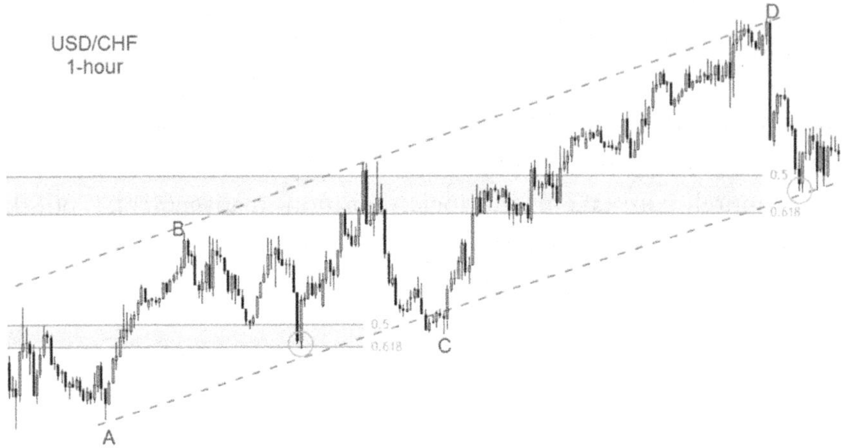

Figure 3.3: Trade Example 1

The first step is always to identify the broader market context. Instead of searching for opportunities inside chaotic price action filled with erratic and unpredictable candles, traders should focus on markets that are moving according to a recognizable structural logic. One of the clearest examples is a stable uptrend where price forms relatively orderly highs and lows, sometimes developing neatly within a parallel channel or gradually ascending structure similar to the one illustrated in Figure 3.3.

This sense of order matters more than many traders realize. When price movement begins displaying rhythm, consistency, and structural balance, it often signals that the market is operating in an environment where behavior becomes easier to interpret and manage. The cleaner the structure, the easier it becomes to identify meaningful retracements, recognize genuine shifts in momentum, and distinguish real continuation setups from random fluctuations.

The next step is to apply the Fibonacci Retracement tool to previous price swings in order to evaluate whether the market is behaving consistently around key retracement areas. When previous pullbacks consistently react around the 0.5 or 0.618 Fibonacci areas, it suggests that these zones are functioning as meaningful support regions where buyers are willing to step back into the market. That recurring behavior matters because it reveals a level of structural discipline within the trend itself.

In the example above, we draw two separate Fibonacci measurements — one from A to B, and another from C to D. Both retracements show clear respect for the Golden Zone, although not with identical precision. The retracement following the A–B swing reacts almost directly from the 0.618 level, while the pullback after the C–D swing stabilizes within the broader 0.5–0.618 zone without reaching the exact 0.618 retracement. This difference is important because it reinforces an idea discussed earlier: Fibonacci should be treated primarily as a zone rather than a collection of exact price levels. Markets often respect areas of pressure more consistently than precise mathematical points, and traders who understand that distinction tend to interpret price behavior far more effectively.

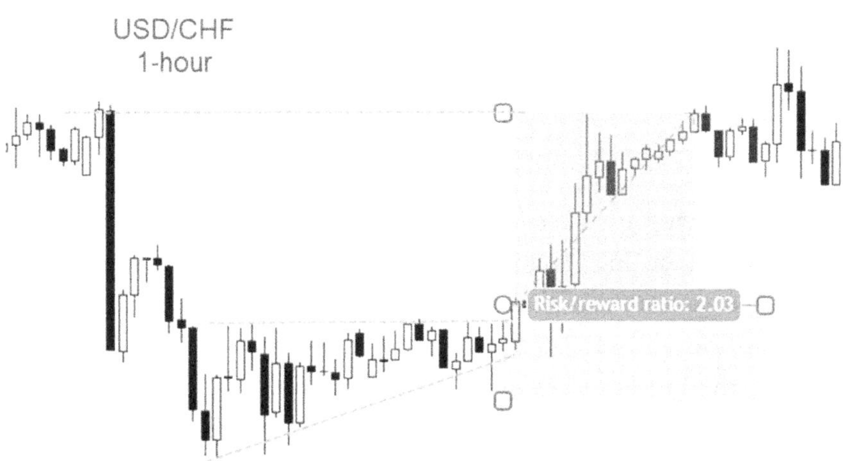

Figure 3.4: Trade Example 1

At the same time, we need to narrow our focus and look for a smaller internal structure developing within the broader market context —

specifically, the consolidation zone forming immediately before the breakout. Rather than relying on a single isolated high, the objective is to identify a compressed sideways structure where price begins tightening beneath resistance. Figure 3.4 presents exactly this type of environment: a prolonged and highly contested battle between Bulls and Bears.

After retracing into the 0.5–0.618 Fibonacci zone, price initially attempts to rebound, but sellers immediately step in to suppress the advance. What follows is a lengthy period of consolidation lasting across many candles, during which the Bears repeatedly defend the upper boundary of the range with clear determination. Their presence is visible each time price approaches resistance and fails to break through decisively. But beneath the surface, the balance of power is gradually beginning to change. Each rejection from the Bears produces a smaller pullback than the one before it. Instead of collapsing lower, price continues forming higher lows as buyers absorb selling pressure underneath the structure. This creates a visible compression pattern where the market becomes increasingly squeezed beneath the multi-top resistance zone. The Bulls are no longer simply reacting to sellers — they are steadily forcing the Bears into a weaker defensive position.

Eventually, that pressure reaches a breaking point. The breakout candle emerges with strong momentum and relatively small upper wicks, pushing decisively through the contested zone after an extended period of exhaustion and repeated defensive effort from the Bears. At that moment, the breakout represents far more than a simple move above resistance. It reflects the conclusion of a prolonged battle in which the selling side gradually lost its ability to maintain control.

At that stage, the official entry is triggered at the closing price of the breakout candle itself. The stop-loss is typically placed just beneath the nearest low inside the compression structure or below the consolidation zone that price has just broken out from, providing enough protection against normal market fluctuations while still maintaining a tight and logical invalidation point.

From there, trade management and profit targets should continue following the same structural logic that supported the setup in the first place. In most cases, the most natural objective remains the 0% Fibonacci level — the prior swing high where the earlier bullish move originally stalled. If that target is unusually far away, partial profit-taking around the 2R level can also be considered before allowing the remaining position to continue toward higher objectives, although situations requiring that adjustment are relatively uncommon in clean trending markets. In the example discussed here, the nearest previous high — point D in Figure 3.3 — also aligns closely with the 2R target, creating a practical and structurally meaningful take-profit area.

One important detail worth emphasizing is that when a trade originates from a market structure with strong internal order and clear compression behavior, the price movement afterward also tends to unfold in a more orderly manner. These types of environments often reduce the likelihood of chaotic stop-loss sweeps and erratic reversals commonly seen in unstable market conditions.

Ultimately, successful trading rarely comes from staring at charts all day searching for random opportunities. It comes from patiently waiting for a specific scenario that has already been studied, understood, and prepared for in advance. When the larger market structure aligns cleanly with the smaller internal structure — particularly the compression and breakout behavior near key Fibonacci zones — the probability of success improves significantly.

Trade Example 2

Building on the ideas of structure and compression discussed earlier, let us examine another real market example — a classic setup on

EUR/GBP. This example highlights an important truth about advanced Fibonacci trading: the technique is not simply about drawing lines on a chart. At its core, it is about understanding the psychology and balance of pressure hidden behind each price movement.

Figure 3.5: Trade Example 2

In this example, we begin by stepping back to a higher timeframe such as the H4 chart in order to evaluate the broader market structure. After an extended bearish trend, price forms the bullish A–B swing and delivers a decisive break above the nearest previous high, signaling that selling pressure is beginning to weaken while buyers gradually regain control of the market (Figure 3.5). This is the moment where the market starts revealing a meaningful structural shift — and where we begin preparing the framework for the setup using Fibonacci.

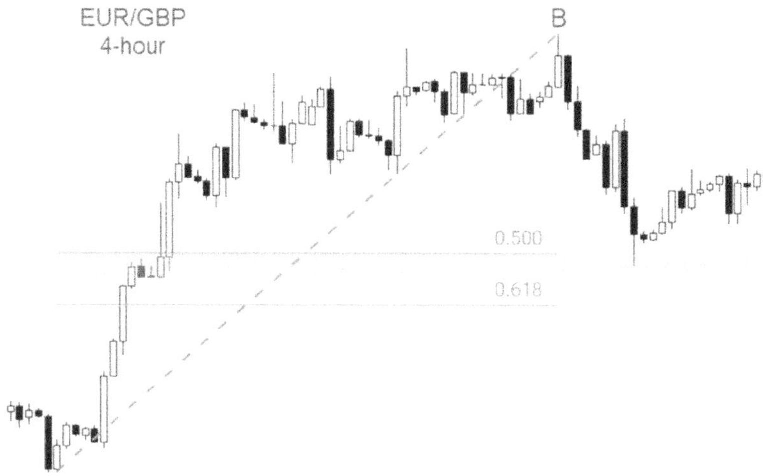

Figure 3.6: Trade Example 2

We then apply the Fibonacci Retracement tool to identify the most favorable pullback area, with the 0.5–0.618 zone remaining the primary region of interest. This is where the previous bullish momentum begins reaching a temporary equilibrium between buying and selling pressure. Once price retraces into this area and starts showing signs of rejection, our attention shifts toward observing the interaction between Bulls and Bears.

Now pay close attention to the highlighted area on the chart during the retracement phase. This zone originates from a cluster of four small-bodied candles that formed earlier during the bullish expansion on the left side of the chart. Structurally, this area is important because it marks the point where buying momentum temporarily stalled as sellers attempted to step into the market. Before those smaller candles appeared, price had already produced three strong bullish candles in succession, showing aggressive buying pressure entering the market. After the brief hesitation, the Bulls regained control and continued driving price higher.

That sequence leaves behind an important footprint. The highlighted area effectively becomes a support zone — a place where buyers previously demonstrated their willingness to defend price before continuing the trend upward. When the later retracement into the 0.5–0.618 Fibonacci zone aligns directly with this prior support structure, the setup gains an additional layer of confluence. The Fibonacci zone is no longer acting alone; it is being reinforced by a structural area where buying pressure has already proven itself in the past.

Returning to the price behavior after the retracement reaches the 0.5–0.618 support zone, the 4-hour chart already reveals signs of conflict developing inside a relatively tight range. Multiple small-bodied candles begin appearing, signaling hesitation and ongoing pressure between buyers and sellers. Structurally, this is an encouraging sign because it suggests that the market is no longer moving impulsively against the trend.

However, another practical issue immediately appears. If we wait for a breakout confirmation directly on the H4 timeframe, the resulting entry may not offer an ideal reward-to-risk profile — especially if the intended profit target remains the previous swing high at point B. This is where multi-timeframe observation becomes extremely useful.

One of the techniques I frequently apply in situations like this is shifting down to a lower timeframe in order to search for a cleaner and more efficient entry structure. In this example, the timeframe selected is the 1-hour chart, where price begins forming a visible sideways consolidation before the breakout eventually takes place.

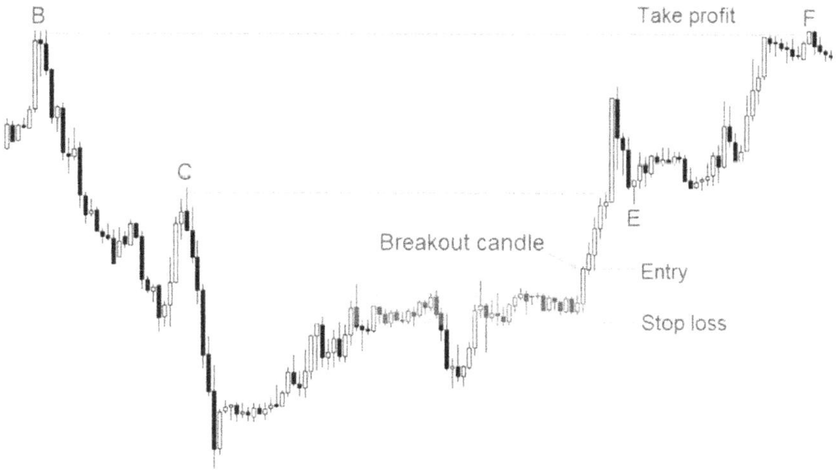

Figure 3.7: Trade Example 2

On Figure 3.7, the battle between Bulls and Bears becomes much easier to recognize because the lower timeframe reveals the internal structure with far greater clarity. From the moment price reaches the Golden Zone, the market begins climbing in a hesitant and uneven manner, alternating between bullish and bearish candles instead of producing a clean impulsive move. This behavior reflects a market where both sides are still actively competing for control, even though the Bulls are gradually beginning to gain a slight advantage.

As price moves deeper into the highly contested area highlighted by the rectangle on the chart, the objective becomes very clear: we wait patiently for the market to resolve the conflict itself. At one point, selling pressure from the Bears even manages to force price temporarily below the rectangle structure. But the breakdown quickly fails, price returns back into the range, and the struggle continues inside an increasingly narrow area. Small candles begin appearing repeatedly, volatility contracts, and the sense of compression intensifies further and further.

Eventually, the pressure reaches its limit. Price breaks above the sideways structure with a decisive bullish candle that closes strongly without leaving a significant upper wick. At that moment, the market finally reveals that buyers have regained control. More importantly, the lower timeframe structure now provides not only a much cleaner entry point, but also a far more logical stop-loss placement — something that would have been difficult to achieve by observing the 4-hour chart alone.

As for profit targets, point F represents the primary objective in this example, corresponding closely to the 0% Fibonacci level at point B. However, before price reaches that target, attention should also be paid to point C, since this area previously triggered a strong bearish reaction and therefore carries the potential for renewed selling pressure. How the trade is managed from this stage depends heavily on the trader's personality, risk tolerance, and overall management style.

- A highly conservative trader may choose to close the entire position at point C in order to secure profits before the market reaches a potentially sensitive resistance area.

- A slightly less conservative trader may prefer taking partial profits instead — for example, closing half the position at point C while allowing the remaining portion of the trade to continue toward the larger target. At that stage, the stop-loss may also be moved to breakeven, although whether that adjustment is appropriate should still depend on the surrounding market conditions.

- Another conservative approach involves using a trailing stop. In this scenario, once price retraces and forms a temporary higher low at point E, the stop-loss can be advanced beneath that structure while still allowing the market enough room to continue toward the projected target at point F.

- A more aggressive trader may choose to observe price behavior at point C without taking immediate profits. In this example, price pauses only briefly through the formation of a relatively small candle before quickly resuming upward momentum with a strong bullish expansion candle. That behavior suggests the Bulls still maintain clear control over the market, making it reasonable to continue holding the position without unnecessary intervention. Price eventually resumes the trend and reaches the projected target at point F.

The most important lesson from this example is not that Fibonacci possesses some kind of magical predictive power. The real lesson lies in understanding how the market behaves around important price zones. Fibonacci simply helps us identify areas worth paying attention to. What matters far more is the ability to read market structure, observe the ongoing battle between Bulls and Bears, and remain patient enough to wait for genuine confirmation before acting.

Trade example 3

In real market conditions, periods of tight consolidation and internal conflict rarely occur only once. Bulls and Bears often pull price through multiple contested zones, creating phases of hesitation and repeated struggle before the market finally produces a breakout strong enough to justify a high-probability entry. Because of that, identifying quality trades requires more than mechanically applying the same formula repeatedly. It demands an understanding of how buying and selling pressure interact within these contested areas and how market structure gradually reveals which side is beginning to gain control.

In this third example, we will go deeper into the process of reading candlestick behavior and structural interaction in order to refine entry selection further. More importantly, the example will also highlight the role of confluence as a second layer of confirmation — an additional source of evidence that strengthens the validity of a potential buying or selling zone.

Figure 3.8: Trade Example 3

Figure 3.8 presents the GBP/USD chart on the 4-hour timeframe. Before searching for any candlestick signal, the first step must always be understanding the broader market structure. In this example, the chart is displaying a clear bullish trend. We focus on the A–B swing shown on the chart — a strong impulsive move that successfully breaks through the previous resistance zones at C and D. Using the Fibonacci Retracement tool, we measure the move from the swing low to the swing high in order to identify the key retracement areas where price may later react.

What makes this setup particularly important is that the 0.5–0.618 Fibonacci zone does not exist in isolation. The retracement area aligns directly with the previous highs that price had already broken above earlier in the trend. Once those highs were breached, the former resistance zone effectively transformed into an important support region where the Bulls would be expected to defend territory on a future pullback.

This convergence creates a much stronger environment than Fibonacci alone could provide. The broader bullish trend, the strength of the impulsive A–B expansion, and the alignment between the Fibonacci retracement zone and the previous breakout structure all combine to reinforce the same area. As a result, the zone becomes highly unfavorable territory for the Bears while simultaneously creating a much more attractive location for potential long positions.

Figure 3.9: Trade Example 3

Figure 3.9 presents the price action as the market retraces into the 0.5–0.618 Fibonacci zone. The highlighted area marks the battlefield where the struggle between buyers and sellers begins unfolding.

As price approaches the predefined buying zone, the candles begin showing hesitation and internal conflict. Sellers continue attempting to push price lower, while buyers repeatedly step in and drive price back toward the upper boundary of the rectangle structure.

Behind every piece of price action, there is a story unfolding between the two sides of the market. A trader's job is not simply to memorize patterns, but to understand the message being communicated through the candles themselves. For me personally, unless the current timeframe is already presenting a very clear narrative through visible compression or repeated sharp reactions between both boundaries of the contested area, I will usually step down to a lower timeframe in order to listen more carefully to the conversation taking place between Bulls and Bears.

So let us move down to the 1-hour chart and examine what the price action there is trying to reveal.

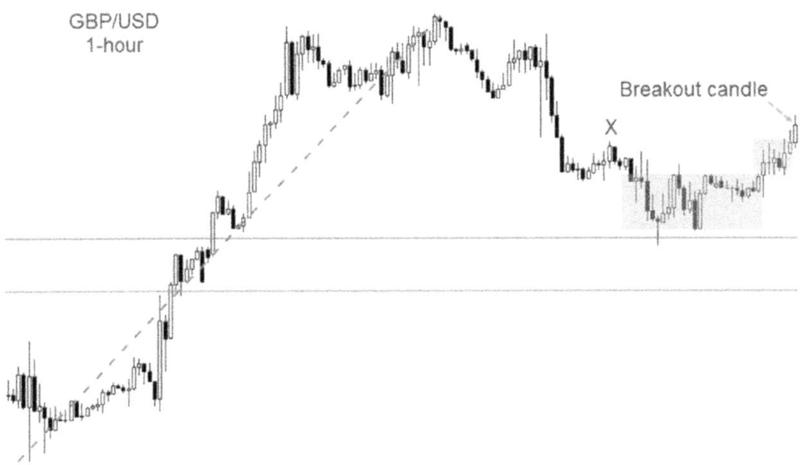

Figure 3.10: Trade Example 3

Figure 3.10 reveals a much clearer narrative once we shift down to the 1-hour timeframe. The retracement itself unfolds in a relatively controlled and gradual manner, and the selling pressure pushing into the Golden Zone is absorbed surprisingly well by the buyers waiting beneath the market. What previously appeared as a single consolidation area on the 4-hour chart now separates into two distinct rectangle structures on the lower timeframe, allowing us to observe the internal battle with far greater detail.

The larger rectangle at the bottom forms during the initial reaction from the Golden Zone. Once price reaches the Fibonacci support area, buyers begin stepping in aggressively enough to stop the decline and generate a rebound. However, the Bears continue applying pressure from above, preventing the market from breaking higher immediately. As a result, price remains trapped inside the rectangle structure for an extended period while the struggle between both sides continues.

But beneath the surface, an important shift gradually begins developing. The Bulls slowly push price upward through the formation of higher lows, creating visible price compression beneath resistance — something that was difficult to recognize clearly on the 4-hour chart alone. This is precisely where multi-timeframe analysis becomes valuable. The higher timeframe shows us the broader context, but the lower timeframe allows us to hear the internal conversation taking place inside the market itself.

At this point, you may be wondering why I did not choose to enter immediately when price first broke above the initial compression structure — especially since the breakout already emerged from a contested zone with visible price compression. In reality, entering at that breakout would still be a completely valid decision. However, my own trading style tends to be more conservative, and this situation provides a good opportunity to demonstrate why reading candlestick behavior and surrounding structure can add another layer of decision-making quality.

Pay close attention to the area marked as zone X. Earlier in the chart, price declined aggressively from this region before falling toward the support zone below. That prior bearish movement suggests the potential presence of remaining sell orders in the area, even if the true strength of that supply is not yet fully visible. In situations like this, I generally prefer waiting for price to break clearly above the zone before entering, because once that overhead resistance is removed, the path for the Bulls becomes significantly cleaner.

Figure 3.10 also reveals that sellers are still attempting to defend zone X even after the first breakout occurs. Price does manage to break above the larger rectangle structure, but instead of accelerating immediately, it begins consolidating once again inside the second rectangle above. That hesitation is meaningful. It tells us the Bears have stepped back into the market and are still trying to slow the advance. In fact, signs of that selling pressure are already visible inside the initial breakout candle itself, which leaves behind a relatively noticeable upper wick compared to the candle body.

At the same time, however, the reaction also reveals something equally important: the Bears are no longer strong enough to force price back down toward the 0.5–0.618 support zone. Instead, the market stabilizes at a much higher level than the previous consolidation area. Structurally, this suggests that buyers are continuing to absorb selling pressure successfully even after the first breakout attempt.

Only when the Bulls finally break through this second contested zone do we obtain the higher-quality entry — specifically at the closing price of the decisive breakout candle shown in Figure 3.10. At that point, the market has not only confirmed the breakout from compression, but also demonstrated that the remaining resistance overhead has been absorbed successfully, creating a much safer continuation setup overall.

Figure 3.11: Trade Example 3

The trade is triggered at the closing price of the breakout candle itself. After an extended period of hesitation filled with repeated rejection candles and failed attempts to push lower, the market finally produces a strong bullish expansion candle. Although the candle still leaves behind a modest upper wick, the decisive close above the consolidation structure — combined with the breakout through the nearest bearish highs — provides enough confirmation to justify a long entry targeting point B, the high of the previous bullish swing.

The trade does encounter some initial resistance shortly after entry, but price ultimately reaches the projected target thanks to the broader bullish context, the support created by the confluence zones beneath the market, and the structural understanding gained from analyzing the interaction between Bulls and Bears across multiple timeframes.

This example reinforces several important ideas simultaneously. First, Fibonacci becomes significantly more powerful when combined with meaningful market structure such as previous support and resistance zones. Second, multi-timeframe analysis often reveals important details that remain hidden on higher timeframes alone, allowing traders to understand the internal narrative behind the price movement instead of relying only on surface-level signals.

More importantly, however, this example highlights the deeper role of candlestick reading itself. Reading candles is not simply about finding entries and exits mechanically. At a higher level, it is about understanding the language of the market — the conversation unfolding between buyers and sellers — so that entries can be timed with greater precision and stronger probability behind them.

I hope this first strategy has helped you become more comfortable combining Fibonacci analysis with price action reading. While the concepts introduced here may appear advanced on the surface, their foundation remains remarkably simple: every movement in the market ultimately comes back to the ongoing struggle between buyers and sellers. And because of that, the principles behind these ideas remain timeless.

CHAPTER 4: EQUILIBRIUM REVERSAL STRATEGY

Up to this point, we have explored the first breakout-based trading examples — setups where entries are confirmed through price breaking out of contested zones after prolonged periods of conflict between Bulls and Bears. In this chapter, we will continue studying market behavior from a different angle by focusing on two of the most familiar reversal candlestick formations in technical analysis: the engulfing pattern and the pin bar pattern.

However, consistent with the broader philosophy of this book, we will not approach these patterns in the conventional way. An engulfing pattern is not important simply because one candle fully covers the previous candle, and a pin bar is not meaningful merely because it has a long wick. What truly matters is the story unfolding behind those candles — the struggle between buyers and sellers taking place at an important price zone.

Throughout this chapter, reversal candlestick patterns will always be analyzed within the context of equilibrium — the phase where price retraces into the 0.5–0.618 Fibonacci zone and the market begins moving through a temporary rebalancing process between supply and demand. Rather than searching for random candlestick formations appearing anywhere on a chart, we will focus specifically on situations where one side gradually begins losing strength, the opposing side starts gaining control, and the candlestick pattern emerges as confirmation that the balance of power is shifting.

The core philosophy remains exactly the same. We still observe consolidation and hesitation. We still pay close attention to how price reacts inside or around the equilibrium zone. And we still remain patient enough to let the market reveal its intentions naturally. The only real difference lies in the trigger itself. In the previous chapter, confirmation came through breakouts above contested structures. In this chapter, the entry trigger will come from reversal candlestick formations instead.

Second Engulfing Pattern (SAP)

Now let us move into the first strategy of this chapter: trading the Second Engulfing Pattern, or SAP. This is a technique I developed through thousands of hours of chart observation and screen time, designed specifically to filter out many of the false signals and psychological traps that traders commonly encounter around reversal setups.

Most traders become overly eager the moment they see a single reversal candle forming at an important area. SAP approaches the market differently. Instead of rushing into a trade based on the first apparent sign of reversal, the strategy demands additional patience and confirmation before committing capital. That patience is important because the market may produce premature reversal signals long before the true shift in control actually takes place.

The Philosophy Behind SAP: Why Wait for the Second Low?

As discussed earlier, one of the most dangerous mistakes traders make is entering immediately after spotting an engulfing candle at the very first low of a retracement. The problem is not the engulfing pattern itself, but the market context surrounding it. At that stage, the side controlling the retracement still usually carries strong momentum. When that pressure is rejected for the first time, it rarely disappears immediately. More often, the dominant side will attempt at least one additional push in order to retest the area and see whether resistance or support can truly hold.

This is the psychological foundation behind the SAP strategy.

The logic is simple: if the opposing side attacks the zone a second time and still fails — especially when that failure is followed by a decisive engulfing pattern — the probability of exhaustion increases dramatically. By that point, the market has already gone through multiple rounds of conflict, and the side attempting to continue the retracement begins losing confidence and momentum. Once control shifts, stop-loss orders trapped on the losing side often start getting triggered in clusters, creating the fuel for a much faster and more aggressive move in the direction of the new dominant side.

SAP Strategy in Details

To integrate SAP into an advanced Fibonacci framework, the process follows four core steps:

- Step 1: Identify the dominant market trend along with an important Fibonacci value zone — typically the 0.5–0.618 retracement area where a reaction may develop.

- Step 2: Observe price as it retraces into that area and forms the first low. In many cases, an engulfing candle may already appear during this initial reaction. However, under the SAP framework, we deliberately avoid entering at this stage.

- Step 3: Wait for the market to perform a second test of the support area and create another low. Importantly, the second low does not need to form at exactly the same level as the first one. It may form slightly higher or slightly lower. The key focus is not geometric perfection, but the gradual exhaustion of one side of the market — in this case, the sellers — while the opposing side begins strengthening its control.

- Step 4: Execute the trade once the second engulfing pattern closes decisively, signaling that momentum has shifted meaningfully in favor of the reversal. The stop-loss is typically placed beneath the second engulfing structure, while profit targets are prioritized around the Fibonacci 0% level or the nearest significant market structure ahead.

Take-profit logic and trade management will be explored in greater detail later in Chapter 6 of this book.

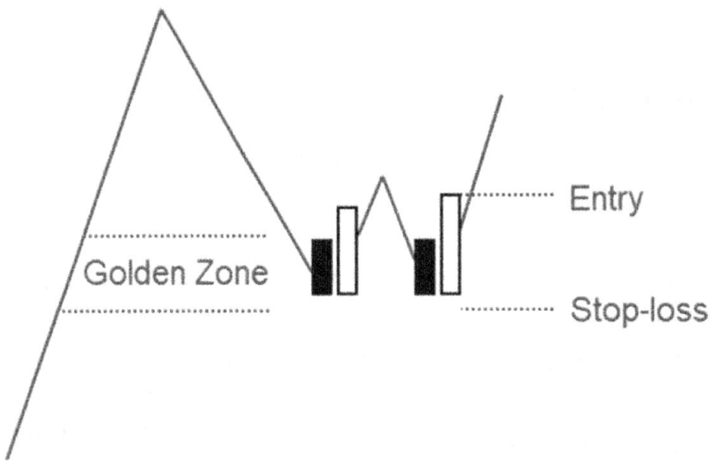

Figure 4.1: SAP strategy

Trade Example 4

Figure 4.2: Trade example 4

Let us begin with the first practical example of the SAP strategy. Figure 4.2 illustrates the 1-hour chart of Tesla stock.

Before this price action structure began forming, the market had already gone through a prolonged bearish phase. Eventually, however, buyers started regaining control, leading to the bullish trend now visible on the chart. The market successfully broke above the nearest swing high responsible for forming the previous swing low structure, signaling that the broader balance of power had begun shifting back toward the Bulls. The bullish expansion itself developed with strong slope and momentum, reflecting aggressive buying pressure entering the market.

What follows next is the retracement phase. Notice that the pullback unfolds in a relatively controlled and gradual manner rather than collapsing aggressively downward. This is important because it suggests that the Bears still possess influence, but their strength remains moderate rather than dominant. At this stage, we apply the Fibonacci Retracement tool to identify the potential support zones around the 0.5 and 0.618 levels, forming the Golden Zone shown on the chart.

Now pay close attention to how price behaves once it enters this trading zone. The market begins reacting to the area through the appearance of an engulfing pattern — the first important clue that buying pressure may be starting to return.

During the market's first test of the Golden Zone at point A, price forms a bearish pin bar with a long upper wick. That candle reveals an important piece of information: buyers initially attempted to push the market higher, but sellers stepped in with even greater force and drove the candle back down aggressively, closing decisively beneath the 0.5 Fibonacci level. Shortly afterward, a bullish engulfing candle appears, fully covering the body of the previous bearish candle. Under normal circumstances, many traders would already view this as a reversal signal and enter immediately.

However, as discussed earlier, SAP intentionally avoids entering on the first engulfing pattern because the selling momentum inside the retracement may still remain strong. In this example, the bearish pin bar itself already hints at that lingering pressure.

And indeed, the market soon pushes lower once again, with the second retracement leg extending toward the 0.618 Fibonacci support level at point B. But this time, the reaction changes dramatically. The moment price reaches the deeper support area, buyers step in aggressively and produce another engulfing pattern — one with enough strength to fully consume the previous bearish candle and signal a much more convincing shift in momentum.

Traders who entered at the close of the first engulfing candle were likely stopped out during the second decline. The ideal SAP entry, however, appears at the close of the second engulfing pattern, with the stop-loss positioned directly beneath the engulfing structure itself.

Now let us unlock the next phase of the price action and examine how the market responds afterward.

Figure 4.3: Trade Example 4

In Figure 4.3, the entry, stop-loss, and take-profit levels are illustrated directly on the chart. As we can see, price reaches the projected target relatively quickly without encountering major difficulty along the way. But the real value of this example lies not only in the successful trade itself, but in the subtle details hidden inside the price action.

The first important area to pay attention to is level Y. Earlier in the chart, this zone acted as support where buyers attempted to defend price before a strong bearish gap candle eventually broke through it, transforming the area into potential resistance. Because of that previous structural role reversal, Y becomes a location where latent selling pressure could reappear and create turbulence during the upward move. However, as shown in the example, price eventually breaks through this level with a strong bullish expansion candle displaying clear momentum and conviction. That candle effectively confirms that buyers still maintain control, giving traders additional confidence to continue holding the position without needing aggressive trade management adjustments.

Another interesting detail appears in the market behavior immediately after entry. Instead of rallying upward instantly, price initially consolidates around the entry area and forms another short period of compression before finally breaking higher through the structure with candle X. The breakout candle closes strongly and decisively, reflecting renewed buying strength and commitment from the Bulls. Structurally, this is the same breakout price action pattern discussed in the previous chapter, now appearing once again within a different strategic context.

In fact, this breakout could also serve as a second valid entry opportunity within the same example, with the stop-loss placed beneath the compression zone itself. The reward-to-risk profile would be slightly less favorable compared to the original SAP entry, but the trade would offer stronger confirmation through additional price action development. In general, SAP tends to provide earlier entries, while breakout-based entries usually offer greater confirmation and therefore a higher sense of security.

Which approach is ultimately preferable — or whether both methods should be combined together — depends entirely on the trader's individual style and risk tolerance.

Trade Example 5

In this second example, we will continue exploring the SAP strategy, but this time through the lens of multi-timeframe analysis. In many situations, SAP structures are hidden beneath the surface of higher timeframes, and traders relying on only a single chart perspective may fail to recognize them completely. Sometimes, a simple shift to a lower timeframe can reveal not only a valid entry setup, but also a far more efficient stop-loss structure capable of improving the overall reward-to-risk profile significantly.

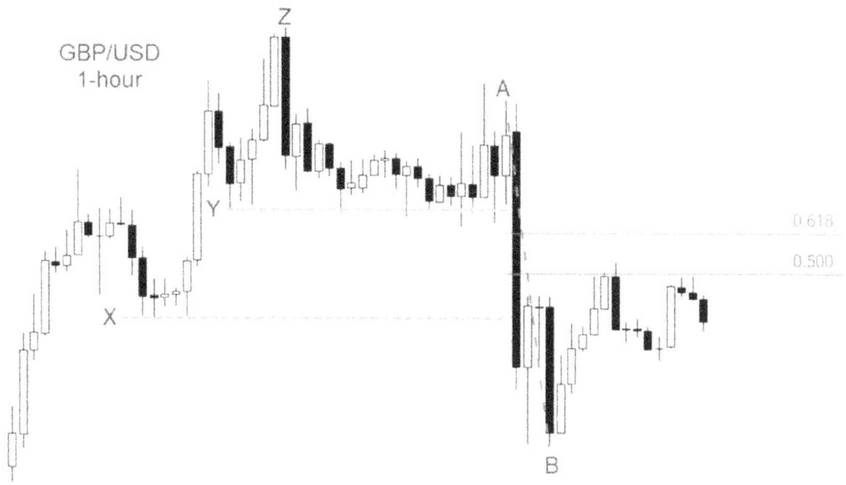

Figure 4.4: Trade Example 5

Figure 4.4 presents the GBP/USD chart on the 1-hour timeframe. Prior to the setup forming, the market had already completed an extended bullish trend and created its highest peak at point Z before sellers stepped in aggressively and began driving price lower. The most striking feature on the chart is the large bearish marubozu candle that closes decisively beneath two important support areas from the previous bullish swing at X and Y. Structurally, this candle carries significant meaning because it reflects strong bearish commitment and signals a potential shift in market control. Price continues declining afterward until reaching point B, where a temporary swing low forms before the market begins retracing upward into the 0.5–0.618 Fibonacci retracement zone.

One important detail worth discussing is the Fibonacci measurement itself. Notice that the retracement grid is drawn from point A to point B rather than from Z to B. In practice, traders may have valid reasons for choosing either approach. Personally, I prefer the A–B swing because it reflects the cleanest and most continuous bearish movement within the structure. The price action between Z and A contains prolonged hesitation, filled with alternating bullish and bearish candles inside a sideways environment. For Fibonacci retracement analysis, the ideal swing should be as clean and smooth as possible. Once a move becomes heavily interrupted by consolidation and overlapping price behavior, the quality of the retracement measurement begins weakening. That is why the A–B leg provides a more reliable foundation for projecting Fibonacci levels in this case.

Returning to Figure 4.4, price retraces upward from point B into the 0.5 Fibonacci level and reacts immediately, forming what appears to be a textbook engulfing pattern. Under normal circumstances, many traders would already enter at this point. But under the SAP framework, our task remains the same: wait patiently for the second engulfing confirmation before committing to the trade.

And indeed, the market does attempt another push back toward the 0.5 Fibonacci area, nearly retesting the level before rolling over again. However, on the 1-hour chart, no obvious second engulfing pattern appears. This is where multi-timeframe analysis becomes extremely valuable. In some situations, the second engulfing structure exists as a hidden signal that only becomes visible on a lower timeframe.

So let us step down to the M15 chart shown in Figure 4.5 and examine what the lower timeframe reveals.

Figure 4.5: Trade Example 5

On the 15-minute timeframe, the SAP structure finally becomes visible once we break down the price action surrounding the market's second return to the 0.5 Fibonacci level from the 1-hour chart. At this stage, the Fibonacci zone effectively becomes the battlefield where buyers and sellers repeatedly test one another for control. However, the advantage clearly belongs to the Bears. Despite multiple retracement attempts from the Bulls, sellers continue defending the Fibonacci level successfully and prevent buyers from achieving even a single convincing close above the area, as illustrated by the arrows on the chart.

The second engulfing formation eventually appears and completely overwhelms the previous bullish attempt, almost like a final rejection of the Bulls' remaining efforts. From there, the entry and stop-loss locations are defined directly on the chart. Profit targets are projected toward the previous swing lows, where buying pressure may potentially re-enter the market and begin absorbing the decline. Price ultimately reaches the 4R target relatively cleanly, but before doing so, one important area deserves attention: support level X.

This level previously acted as a defensive base for the Bulls, meaning latent buying pressure could still emerge there and create temporary resistance against the downward move. However, the bearish expansion candle that breaks through support X closes with strong conviction, providing a clear sign that sellers still maintain control. That decisive close gives traders enough confidence to continue holding the position without needing immediate defensive trade management adjustments such as partial profit-taking.

At the same time, the long-wick candles appearing afterward also create opportunities for more conservative traders to trail stop-loss positions gradually while still allowing the trade enough room to benefit from the ongoing bearish momentum.

As you can see, reading candlesticks, understanding market behavior, and applying multi-timeframe analysis allow us to participate in the market with confidence without turning trading into something unnecessarily complicated. At its core, trading always comes back to one fundamental question: at this moment, which side truly controls the market? When an SAP structure appears around a Golden Fibonacci zone, it often serves as one of the clearest confirmations that one side is beginning to surrender while the other takes control decisively. The goal is to practice until recognizing these situations becomes instinctive, because in trading, knowledge only becomes truly valuable once it has been absorbed deeply enough to operate naturally under pressure.

At the same time, an important concern naturally arises here. By waiting for the second engulfing candle, we may miss certain trades. In reality, markets do not always return for a second test of a Fibonacci zone before reversing, and moving down to lower timeframes will not always reveal a hidden SAP structure either. That is simply part of trading, and it is something we must accept.

But the trade-off is meaningful. By demanding additional confirmation, we also avoid many unnecessary stop-outs caused by entering too early before one side has genuinely exhausted itself and before the opposing side has clearly established dominance. In trading and investing alike, protecting your account is always the highest priority. Avoiding unnecessary losses matters not only financially, but psychologically as well. Many damaging emotional habits in trading begin accumulating quietly through repeated avoidable losses that slowly erode discipline, confidence, and decision-making quality over time.

That is why every strategy presented throughout this book is ultimately designed around the same objective: preserving clarity, discipline, and long-term consistency rather than chasing constant market activity. High trading frequency is not the goal. Sustainable execution is.

I hope the broader philosophy behind SAP is becoming clearer now, and that you continue practicing the strategy patiently and consistently until you begin experiencing its real strength firsthand. With that foundation in place, let us move on to the second strategy in this chapter — a deeper approach to optimizing the effectiveness of the pin bar pattern.

Pin Bar Cluster (PBC)

If the first strategy in this chapter can be viewed as an upgraded version of the traditional engulfing pattern, then the strategy in this section is built around another extremely familiar formation: the pin bar.

The essence of a pin bar lies in its wick. A long upper wick reveals that buyers attempted to push price higher but were ultimately overwhelmed by sellers before the candle closed. A long lower wick tells the opposite story — sellers tried forcing price downward but failed under the counterattack from buyers. In both cases, a pin bar represents evidence of conflict. It is the footprint left behind when one side attempted to seize control of the market and failed.

But a single pin bar alone is rarely enough to justify action. One failed attempt does not necessarily mean surrender. The losing side within that candle may regroup, return to the same area, and launch another attack — sometimes multiple times. Entering immediately after the first pin bar often means committing capital while the battle itself is still unresolved.

This is precisely why the strategy introduced here does not rely on isolated pin bars. What we are looking for instead is a pin bar cluster.

It is also important to recognize that this setup tends to appear less frequently than many of the other strategies discussed throughout this book, particularly in stock markets where price behavior often develops differently from forex environments.

The Psychology Behind the Pin Bar Cluster

A pin bar cluster is a sequence of multiple pin bars forming around the same important support or resistance zone, with the candle wicks pointing in the same direction. For the signal to carry meaningful weight, the cluster should contain at least three candles. That number is not arbitrary. The first rejection represents an initial test. The second reflects persistence. The third begins confirming that the losing side is no longer simply pausing, but is genuinely becoming exhausted. The longer the wicks and the greater the number of pin bars inside the cluster, the more aggressively the market is rejecting that price area.

Psychologically, a cluster tells a much clearer story than a single candle ever could. One side of the market has attempted to break through the zone not once, but repeatedly — and each attempt has failed, with price being pushed back immediately every time. That repetition creates something extremely important: evidence of a process. Not just a beautiful momentary signal, but the visible conclusion of an extended battle that is gradually producing a winner and a loser.

PBC Strategy in Details

To apply the PBC strategy within an advanced Fibonacci framework, we follow a structured four-step process:

- Step 1: Identify the dominant market trend along with an important Fibonacci value area — typically the 0.5–0.618 retracement zone where a reaction is likely to develop.

- Step 2: Observe price as it retraces into that area and forms the initial low or high. At this stage, a reversal pin bar may already appear, but under the PBC framework, we deliberately avoid entering immediately.

- Step 3: Patiently monitor the struggle between Bulls and Bears as a cluster begins forming — ideally at least three consecutive pin bars showing repeated rejection around the Golden Fibonacci zone. The goal is not to react to a single candle, but to observe the gradual exhaustion of one side through repeated failed attempts.

- Step 4: Trigger the trade once a decisive candle closes beyond the contested area in the opposite direction of the pin bar wicks, provided the setup still offers a minimum reward-to-risk ratio of at least 1.5. The stop-loss is placed beneath the breakout candle structure, while profit targets are prioritized around the Fibonacci 0% level or the nearest significant market structure ahead.

We will explore take-profit logic and trade management techniques in much greater detail later in Chapter 6 of this book.

Trade Example 6

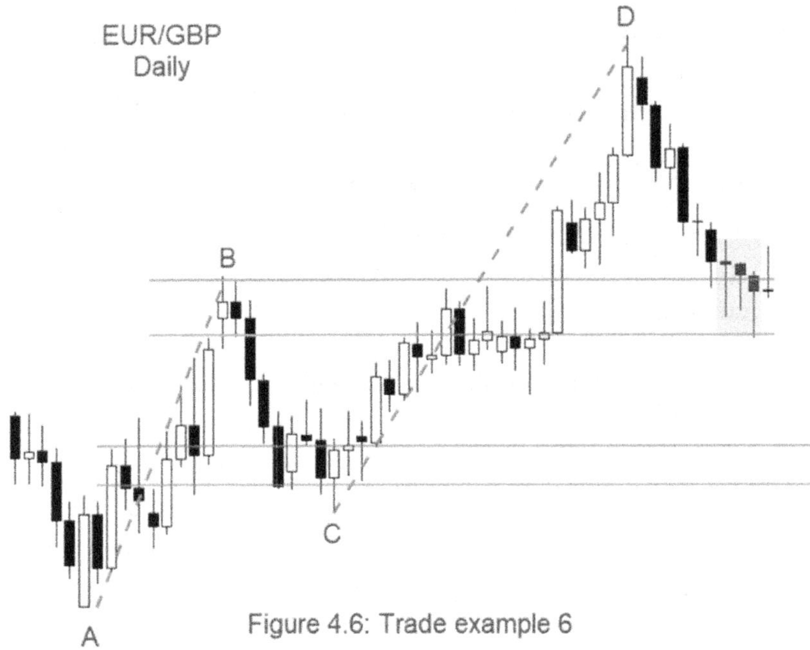

Figure 4.6: Trade example 6

Let us begin with the first example using the EUR/GBP daily chart. In this case, the market is clearly trending upward, consistently forming higher highs and higher lows throughout the structure. The pair itself provides an excellent example of clean and well-organized price action. After completing the bullish impulse swings A–B and later C–D, price retraces naturally into the 0.5–0.618 Fibonacci zone of the preceding bullish leg, creating a rhythmically balanced market structure that is highly favorable for Fibonacci-based analysis.

Now focus on the retracement that develops after the C–D swing is completed. The 0.5–0.618 Fibonacci zone aligns directly with the previous resistance area around point B. Structurally, this zone carries important meaning because it was previously defended by the Bears before the Bulls eventually managed to break above it and establish control. In other words, what was once bearish territory has now become a defensive base for the Bulls. Because of that transition, when price later retraces back into the area, buyers naturally have strong incentive to step in and protect their newly established territory.

And that is exactly what begins happening. As price enters the Golden Zone, repeated rejection candles with long lower wicks start appearing one after another. Buyers begin counterattacking as early as the 0.5 Fibonacci level, and once price reaches the deeper 0.618 support area, the bullish response becomes even more aggressive, forming a visible cluster of long-wick rejection candles. Within this context, our task is not to enter immediately, but to wait patiently for a decisive breakout candle capable of resolving the struggle between both sides.

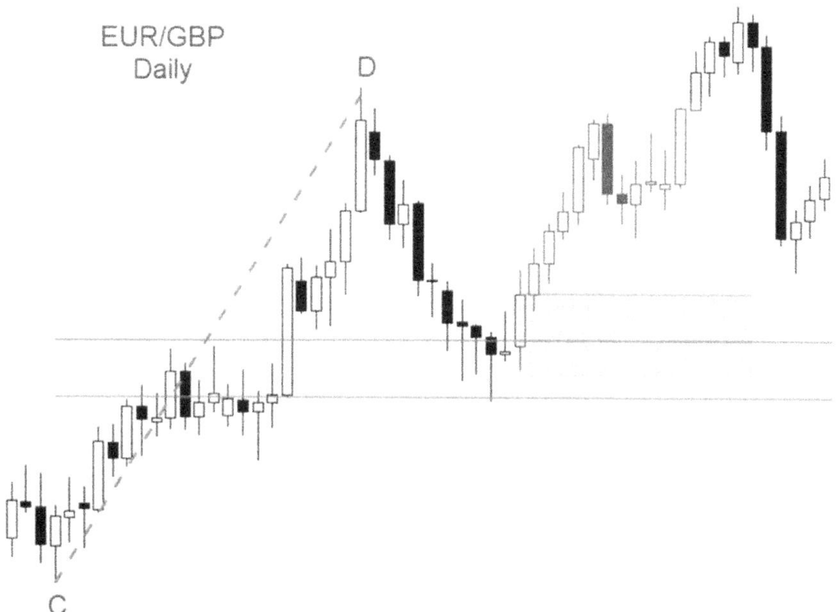

Figure 4.7: Trade example 6

In Figure 4.7, the trade entry is triggered once a bullish candle emerges with enough strength to break through the previous consolidation structure. By this stage, the story behind the price action has become much clearer. Sellers have already made repeated attempts to push the market lower, but buyers continue absorbing the pressure and gradually forcing the Bears backward step by step. The balance of power finally shifts decisively when the Bulls reclaim control through a strong expansion candle that closes firmly above the contested area formed by the earlier cluster of candles.

Equally important, however, is the quality of the breakout candle itself. The candle should display strength and conviction, but it should not become excessively large with an oversized body or wick. If the breakout candle stretches too aggressively, the resulting reward-to-risk ratio often becomes less attractive. In this example, targeting the nearest key level still provides a reward-to-risk ratio close to 2R, which is more than sufficient to justify taking the trade confidently.

With this strategy, there will also be situations where the dominant side wins so aggressively that the breakout candle closes far above the contested zone and approaches the nearest key level almost immediately. In those cases, whether to enter or not becomes more dependent on individual trading style. On one hand, the market is clearly showing strong momentum and decisive control. On the other hand, the remaining distance toward the nearest take-profit level may no longer provide an attractive reward-to-risk profile.

More aggressive traders may still choose to participate in such setups by taking partial profits at the nearest key level — often the Fibonacci 0% level — while leaving the remaining portion of the position open in anticipation that the momentum could continue carrying price significantly further. This approach can still be applied even when the distance from the entry point to the Fibonacci 0% take-profit level already provides an R:R ratio of 1.5 or greater, allowing traders to continue taking advantage of any remaining bullish momentum. Of course, as I mentioned earlier, the decision ultimately depends on each trader's individual style and risk tolerance. I will discuss this topic in greater detail in Chapter 6 of the book.

Trade Example 7

In this next example, I want to broaden the perspective around the PBC strategy slightly. By now, you may already notice that pin bar clusters do not always appear as perfectly consecutive candles lined up one after another. In many real market situations, the rejection wicks may be separated by several candles in between while still preserving the essential characteristic of the setup: repeated rejection occurring around the same important zone. As long as there are at least three meaningful rejection wicks and they collectively form a clear area of conflict between Bulls and Bears, the underlying logic of the strategy remains valid.

What truly matters is not visual perfection, but the evidence of an ongoing struggle where one side repeatedly fails to push through a critical area. Once price finally breaks beyond that consolidation and rejection structure, the probability of trend continuation often increases significantly.

In the following example, we will examine more closely how these rejection wicks develop over time and, more importantly, how they can help create a more advantageous stop-loss placement for the trade itself.

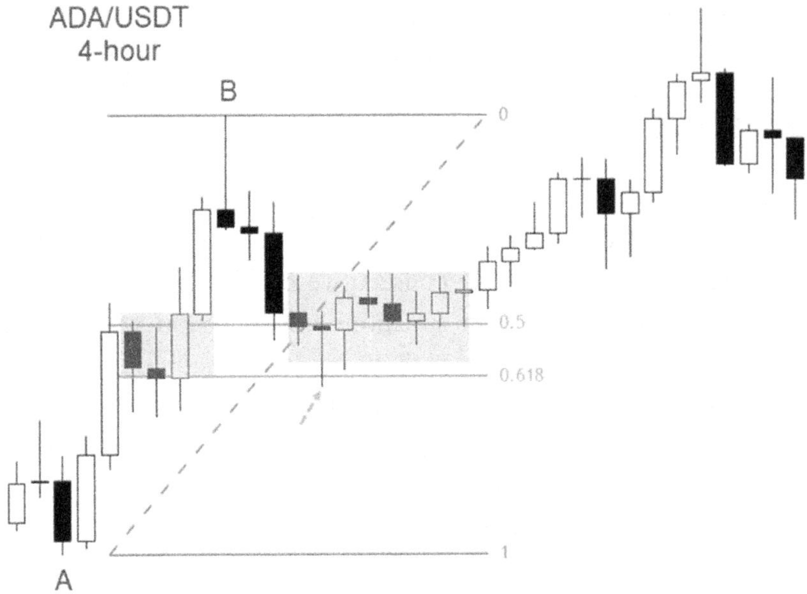

Figure 4.8: Trade example 7

Figure 4.8 presents the Cardano 4-hour chart, where the market remains within a broader bullish trend. Two important zones are highlighted using rectangles on the chart, and each of them reveals a different layer of information about the ongoing battle between buyers and sellers.

The first zone, located on the left side of the chart, represents a brief but meaningful struggle that occurred during the earlier bullish expansion. Inside this area, three candles form a small contested structure, with the third candle attempting to break upward through the previous bearish pressure. Although that breakout candle still leaves behind a somewhat noticeable upper wick — signaling that sellers were resisting aggressively — the market ultimately succeeds in pushing above the area. Structurally, once a contested zone like this is broken to the upside, it often transforms into a potential support region during future retracements. That is precisely why the later pullback into the 0.5–0.618 Fibonacci zone becomes particularly attractive: the Fibonacci retracement area aligns directly with this previous battle zone, creating meaningful confluence for traders searching for buying opportunities.

The second zone, located on the right side of the chart, reveals a longer and more intense struggle between Bulls and Bears. Multiple candles form long lower wicks throughout the structure. While the pin bars are not perfectly consecutive, they collectively create a very clear cluster of repeated rejection inside a well-defined rectangular range. From a PBC perspective, this absolutely qualifies as a valid contested zone because the essential requirement is not perfect candle sequencing, but repeated evidence that sellers continue failing to force the market lower.

Across the entire structure, there are eight candles in total. Among them, the second candle — marked by the arrow — is especially important. It reflects a strong bearish attempt to push price down toward the 0.618 Fibonacci level. However, the buying pressure waiting there proves overwhelming, aggressively rejecting the decline and forcing price back upward toward the 0.5 level. This becomes a genuinely meaningful pin bar because it demonstrates clear rejection from a critical support zone.

The following candle reinforces the message even further. It forms another pin bar and closes decisively above the 0.5 Fibonacci level, creating an important structural shift inside the battle itself. From that moment onward, price begins maintaining stability above the 0.5 retracement area. In fact, during the next five candles inside the rectangle, the market can no longer achieve a close beneath that level — a subtle but extremely important sign that the Bulls are gradually taking control of the battlefield.

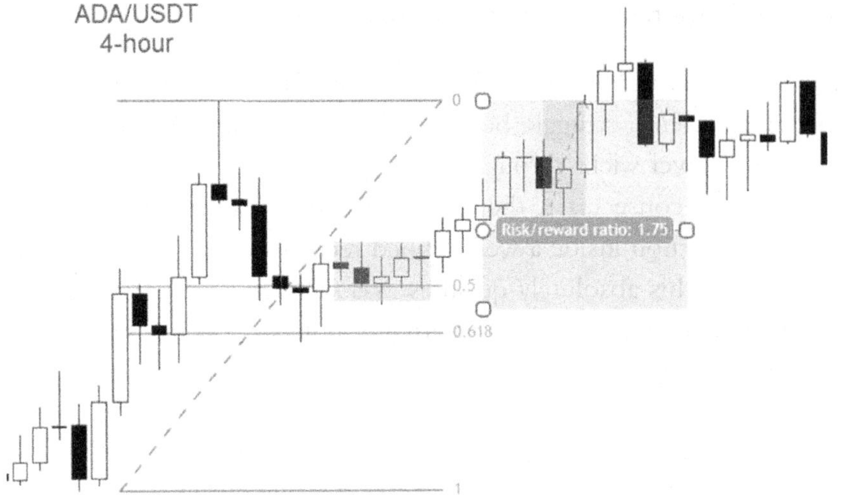

Figure 4.9: Trade example 7

This structural shift gives us an important advantage when it comes to stop-loss placement, as illustrated in Figure 4.9. Instead of positioning the stop-loss beneath the lowest wick formed during the entire consolidation process — which would place it below the 0.618 Fibonacci level — we can now use the smaller upper consolidation structure as our protective boundary. In other words, the stop-loss only needs to sit beneath the higher contested zone that emerged after the internal battle between Bulls and Bears had already begun shifting in favor of the buyers.

That distinction matters because it allows the trade to maintain a tighter risk profile without sacrificing structural logic. The market has already demonstrated that buyers are capable of defending price above the 0.5 Fibonacci level repeatedly, making the lower part of the overall retracement structure less relevant for invalidation purposes.

Using this approach, the setup still achieves a reward-to-risk ratio of approximately 1.75 even if the profit target is limited to the Fibonacci 0% level — the previous high at point B. Admittedly, the resulting R:R may not appear as attractive as some more aggressive trading methods. But that trade-off reflects the nature of this strategy itself: sacrificing a portion of potential reward in exchange for greater confirmation, higher structural reliability, and a stronger overall probability of success.

Trade Example 8

One thing that is not mandatory — but that I strongly encourage — is learning how to combine the strategies presented throughout this book together naturally. I often describe this as developing a kind of trading reflex: an unconscious ability to recognize how different concepts reinforce one another in real market conditions. We will explore this idea more deeply near the end of the book.

But that reflex cannot be forced artificially. It only develops after you have spent enough time practicing each strategy individually until the logic behind them becomes internalized. The important thing is to avoid overcomplicating the process prematurely. Trying too hard to combine every concept mechanically often leads to hesitation, confusion, and unnecessary complexity in execution.

Let us move on to the next example to understand this idea more concretely.

Figure 4.10: Trade example 8

Let us now examine the Bitcoin 4-hour chart. The market forms a clean bullish expansion followed by a retracement back into the 0.5–0.618 Fibonacci zone, which also aligns with a strong preexisting support area. Similar to the previous example, an intense battle develops inside this region. However, the Bulls continue maintaining the upper hand by successfully preventing the Bears from achieving any decisive candle close beneath the 0.618 Fibonacci level.

The dominance of the buyers becomes even more visible when a large bullish candle appears with a long lower wick but an even stronger body, closing decisively above the contested structure formed by the previous four candles — the candle highlighted on the chart. Structurally, the message from the market is very clear: sellers attempted to push lower, failed repeatedly, and buyers eventually regained control aggressively.

However, despite the quality of the breakout itself, there is an important practical issue here. If we enter directly at the close of this candle while applying the same stop-loss and take-profit principles discussed earlier, the resulting reward-to-risk ratio would fail to reach the minimum 1.5

threshold. Because of that, I generally would not recommend taking the trade in this form.

This is precisely the type of situation mentioned at the end of the previous example — a breakout candle that looks extremely strong but closes too far away from the underlying consolidation zone, reducing the attractiveness of the trade from a risk management perspective. And this is where flexibility and strategic reflex begin becoming important. We shift our attention toward the other strategies introduced earlier and ask a more useful question: is there another way to approach this setup more efficiently?

Now let us observe how price evolves afterward in Figure 4.10. Instead of rallying upward immediately after the breakout candle, the market performs a shallow pullback to retest the demand zone around the 0.5–0.618 Fibonacci retracement levels. The moment price revisits this area, buyers step in aggressively once again and produce a high-quality engulfing candle, clearly signaling renewed bullish intent at the support zone.

At this stage, several important elements have now aligned together simultaneously:

- A classic double-bottom structure.
- Repeated bullish rejection through the series of long lower-wick candles formed around the first bottom — the PBC pattern.
- A bullish engulfing pattern forming at the second bottom.

What we are seeing here is no longer just a single isolated signal. It is the combination of multiple layers of confirmation reinforcing the same underlying narrative. The repeated rejection wicks reveal that buyers have consistently absorbed selling pressure at this key support area, while the engulfing pattern at the second bottom confirms that the Bulls are beginning to regain initiative more decisively.

Under this context, the engulfing candle becomes a highly attractive trigger for entry at its closing price. Structurally, the Bears are beginning to lose control step by step while the Bulls steadily reclaim dominance over the battlefield — exactly as illustrated later in Figure 4.11.

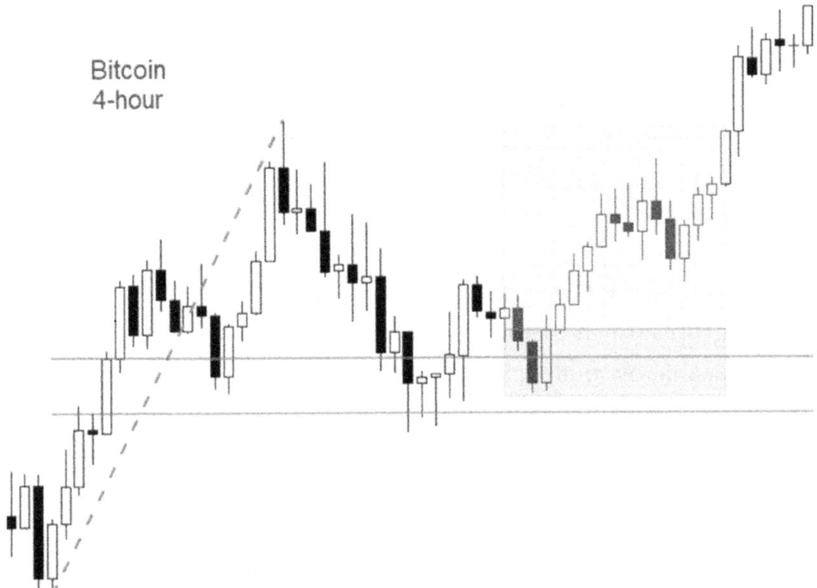

Figure 4.11: Trade example 8

By remaining patient just a little longer, the setup transforms into a trade offering a reward-to-risk ratio of nearly 3R — an exceptionally attractive profile when using the nearest key level, namely the Fibonacci 0% level, as the primary take-profit target.

And yet, this still is not the only possible way to combine the concepts presented so far. Let us step down to the 1-hour timeframe and see what additional opportunity the market has quietly prepared beneath the surface.

Figure 4.12: Trade example 8

Figure 4.12 reveals how the same price behavior unfolds on the 1-hour timeframe. On this chart, the long lower wicks that appeared somewhat abstract on the 4-hour candles now become much clearer and easier to interpret through the formation of a highly contested consolidation structure with visible price compression. The compression zone gradually develops higher lows, signaling that buying pressure is steadily increasing beneath the market and that the Bulls are beginning to squeeze the Bears into a weaker position.

The entry is triggered once a bullish candle closes decisively above the compression structure. Structurally, this breakout provides a much tighter invalidation point while still targeting the same higher timeframe objective, resulting in a reward-to-risk ratio of approximately 3.5R — even better than the earlier engulfing-pattern entry discussed previously.

Once again, this example highlights how multi-timeframe analysis can uncover hidden opportunities that remain invisible on higher timeframes alone. And as I mentioned earlier, this process eventually becomes natural with enough screen time and market experience. Over time, traders begin developing an intuitive sense for what may be happening beneath the surface of the higher timeframe candles and what types of structures are likely forming on the lower timeframes.

That familiarity comes from repetition. In trading, experience often matters less because of how much information you consciously remember, and more because repeated exposure gradually trains your eyes and instincts to recognize meaningful behavior automatically. That is why people say that practice eventually becomes second nature.

The Philosophy of "Trading With Your Ass" – Discipline as the Ultimate Edge

With that, the PBC method brings Chapter 4 to a close, marking the final strategy in this section built around equilibrium market conditions — environments where the market searches for deeper retracements before continuing the broader trend. These are market structures that demand an exceptional level of patience from traders. And because of that, I want to end this chapter with a concept that has become deeply important in my own trading philosophy: "trading with your ass."

What this really means is that when you sit in front of the chart, you should no longer need to overanalyze, overinterpret, or constantly invent explanations for every movement. All the thinking, logic, and trading rules should already have been prepared beforehand through extensive backtesting and deliberate practice. By that stage, the process has become reflexive.

Once the market begins moving, your only job is to sit still, remain disciplined, and observe whether price is unfolding according to the scenario you already planned for. A truly high-quality setup should feel so clear that you do not need to hesitate for even a second once it finally appears.

Train your eyes to become sensitive to the "turns" in market behavior. Learn to place yourself mentally on both sides of the battlefield — alongside the Bulls and alongside the Bears — so that you can sense which side is genuinely controlling the market at any given moment. In the end, trading is not a competition to predict exact tops and bottoms. It is a game of patience, discipline, and waiting for moments where the odds are already tilted in your favor before you act.

CHAPTER 5: MOMENTUM BREAKOUT STRATEGY

There are stretches of river where the current slows down, bends gently, and gives the leaf enough time to find its position before continuing downstream. Those are the deeper retracement environments discussed throughout the previous chapters — situations where price returns into the Fibonacci equilibrium zone around 0.5–0.618, where Bulls and Bears struggle long enough to leave behind clear footprints, and where traders are given enough time to observe the battle before making a decision.

But not every part of the river behaves that way.

Sometimes the current moves so aggressively that hesitation barely has room to exist. Price pulls back only slightly — touching the 0.236–0.382 Fibonacci zone before resuming the trend, or consolidating above those shallow retracement levels without ever reaching the deeper Fibonacci areas at all. It feels as though the dominant flow simply has no interest in resting for long. These situations are often signs of a high-trending market environment: the opposing side attempts to force a deeper retracement, but lacks the strength necessary to pull price down meaningfully. The momentum of the dominant side remains too powerful to allow the market to retrace beyond roughly one-third of the previous impulse wave.

In this chapter, we will continue combining Fibonacci analysis with price action, breakout structures, and localized consolidation behavior in order to identify high-probability continuation setups. The difference now lies in the market context itself. Momentum becomes a more dominant force, meaning traders must adapt to shallower retracements, and a different style of expectation management compared to the equilibrium-based setups explored earlier in the book.

Momentum and Shallow Retracements

Price does not always retrace deeply into the Fibonacci 0.5–0.618 zone and patiently give us time to observe, prepare, and position ourselves. During strongly trending market conditions — when the dominant side still possesses overwhelming momentum — pullbacks can become remarkably shallow, sometimes reacting only around the 0.236–0.382 Fibonacci region before immediately resuming the trend.

Under these conditions, Fibonacci no longer functions primarily as a tool for locating traditional entry or exit points. Instead, it becomes a tool for measuring momentum. A shallow retracement is the market's way of revealing that the main current remains powerful — that this pullback is merely a brief pause before the dominant trend resumes its movement.

In these environments, what we continue looking for is a compression structure followed by a breakout from that compression. By the time price consolidates above the shallow Fibonacci zone, two sources of energy are beginning to build simultaneously: the existing momentum of the dominant side has not disappeared, while the consolidation itself creates additional pressure through the tightening struggle between buyers and sellers. When both forces are finally released together through a decisive breakout candle escaping the compressed range, the continuation move often becomes significantly faster and more explosive than a standard trend-following entry.

Of course, that does not mean every breakout automatically deserves our trust. There are still situations where caution becomes necessary. The first occurs when the dominant trend has already extended for too long. In those cases, momentum may be approaching the later stages of its cycle, increasing the probability of structural reversal or prolonged sideways behavior. The second occurs when an important opposing key level sits too close to the breakout candle itself. In that situation, price may not have enough space to travel before encountering resistance again, weakening the reward-to-risk profile and increasing the likelihood of reversal.

Later in this chapter, we will examine an example where price no longer has sufficient room to continue meaningfully after the breakout — followed by a deeper discussion on the art of turning a losing situation into a winning one.

Momentum Breakout Strategy

The strategy built around shallow Fibonacci retracements does not require a large number of conditions — but the conditions it does require must align properly. The core idea is remarkably straightforward: momentum remains strong, price produces only a shallow pullback followed by consolidation, and we wait for the precise moment when that compressed energy is released so we can enter alongside the dominant side of the market.

To make the structure easier to visualize, the first step is to add one additional level to your Fibonacci Retracement tool: the -0.236 level, as illustrated in Figure 5.1 below. This extra level will help clarify the logic behind the strategy and provide a cleaner framework for understanding the continuation targets discussed throughout this chapter.

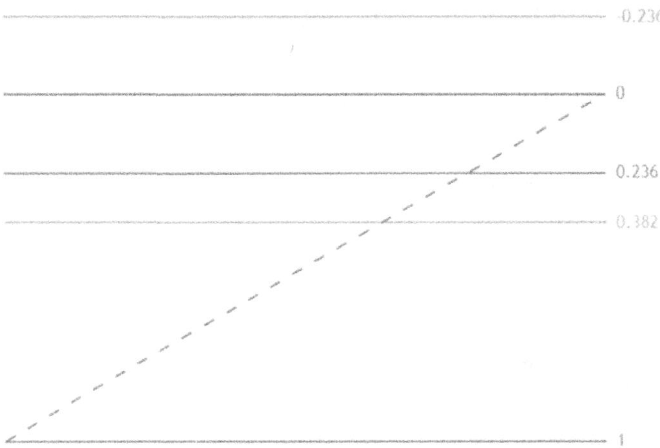

Figure 5.1: Fibonacci retracement and extension

Entry

Figure 5.2: Entry level

The entry is triggered at the closing price of the breakout candle escaping the consolidation structure, as illustrated in Figure 5.2.

One important characteristic of this strategy is that the consolidation zone itself is not strictly confined within the traditional 0%–0.382 Fibonacci range. Price is fully allowed to break above the previous high — meaning above the 0% Fibonacci level — while the setup still remains valid, provided the market does not extend beyond the -0.236 Fibonacci level.

The reason for extending the observation zone toward the -0.236 extension is to take advantage of the momentum that often appears once price breaks above the previous high. Structurally, this is frequently the phase where bullish pressure becomes strongest and continuation probability increases significantly. However, the limitation at the -0.236 level is intentional. Once price extends too far beyond that point, the setup no longer belongs purely to the momentum-based Fibonacci narrative discussed in this strategy. Other market variables begin interfering with the structure, the quality of the setup starts deteriorating, and the statistical advantage provided by the strategy itself becomes far less reliable.

From my experience, there are several important details worth paying attention to when evaluating entries within this strategy:

- First, the consolidation structure itself should appear balanced and orderly. Ideally, the trading range gradually tightens over time, creating visible compression. At minimum, the structure should contain at least two clearly identifiable highs, while avoiding candles with excessively long wicks violently piercing outside the range. Oversized wicks often signal instability and chaotic price behavior rather than true compression — and it is compression, not chaos, that creates reliable breakout energy.

- Second, the breakout candle should be decisive, but it should not explode excessively far away from the consolidation zone. If the breakout extends too aggressively from the structure, the resulting reward-to-risk profile usually becomes less attractive because the entry occurs too late relative to the underlying support base.

- Third, the closing price of the breakout candle should not sit too close to a significant opposing key level ahead. If the available price space becomes too limited, the market may lack sufficient room to continue moving before encountering resistance again, increasing the probability of rejection or reversal and weakening the overall quality of the trade.

Stop Loss

The stop-loss should be placed beneath the consolidation structure itself — specifically below the lowest point of the contested candle cluster. This placement provides enough room to avoid being caught by short-term liquidity sweeps while still remaining tight enough to preserve a healthy reward-to-risk ratio.

Take-Profit

Under this strategy, the take-profit target is no longer centered around the Fibonacci 0% level itself. Instead, priority is given to the next significant key level located beyond the previous high — the area where the opposing side is most likely to regroup and create meaningful resistance again. If no obvious key level exists nearby, or if the next structural level is located unusually far away, then targeting a reward-to-risk ratio around 2R becomes a practical alternative.

From my own trading experience, a 2R target tends to provide a healthy balance between realism and profitability. It offers enough room to withstand normal market noise and temporary fluctuations while still maintaining strong long-term expectancy across a large sample of trades.

The details surrounding take-profit logic and trade management will be explored more thoroughly later in Chapter 6 of this book.

Trade Example 9

Let us begin with the first example illustrating this strategy. I specifically chose this setup because it represents one of the most classic and desirable scenarios traders hope to encounter when working with consolidation structures and breakout continuation patterns.

By now, we already understand that the goal is to wait for price to break out from a compressed consolidation zone — and that the structure should ideally contain at least two relatively equal highs. As discussed earlier in Chapter 3, the existence of multiple equal highs reveals something important beneath the surface: sellers have repeatedly attempted to step in and halt the bullish advance, yet each effort ultimately failed.

Every additional defense consumes more energy from the opposing side. The more times the Bears are forced to fight unsuccessfully around the same resistance zone, the more exhausted their resources gradually become. And when those repeated defensive efforts still fail to stop the advance, the path for the Bulls often becomes significantly easier afterward, allowing price to continue pushing higher with greater momentum.

Figure 5.3: Trade example 9

Figure 5.3 presents the gold price on the 4-hour timeframe. From the broader perspective, the market remains firmly inside a strong uptrend, while the section of price action shown here reflects a continuation phase developing after a relatively short consolidation period. We apply the Fibonacci Retracement tool to the A–B impulse wave in order to identify potential retracement zones where the trend may resume.

What immediately stands out is the strength of the bullish momentum. Price retraces only into the shallow 0.236–0.382 Fibonacci zone before quickly recovering back toward the 0% level. Once price returns to that area, selling pressure begins appearing and creates a contested consolidation structure with two relatively equal highs, while the lows gradually rise over time, producing an ideal compression pattern.

So why do I consider compression forming around the 0% level particularly attractive? Put simply, it creates a kind of momentum confluence. We already understand that point B previously acted as a swing high. Therefore, when price eventually breaks not only out of the consolidation itself but also through the prior swing high, the breakout gains additional significance. Even if that swing high is not an especially major structural level, the very act of overcoming it still strengthens the probability that price can continue traveling further afterward.

The logic behind this comes directly from the ongoing battle between Bulls and Bears. The more important a defensive structure is, the more meaningful it becomes when that structure is finally broken. A successful breakout through a previously defended zone signals that the attacking side possesses genuine strength. You can naturally extend this idea even further: if the price history surrounding swing high B contains multiple prior highs or lows at roughly the same area, then the 0% Fibonacci level becomes even more structurally important. And if price successfully breaks through that key level, continuation potential increases substantially because the breakout candle is no longer escaping only a small consolidation — it is simultaneously breaking through a larger higher-timeframe barrier as well.

The entry, stop-loss, and take-profit levels are illustrated directly on the figure. In this example, the take-profit target is fixed at 2R because there are no major key levels immediately above the entry area, while the next meaningful resistance zones remain relatively far away from current price. As the chart demonstrates, once the breakout is triggered, price reaches the target relatively cleanly without encountering significant resistance along the way.

Trade Example 10

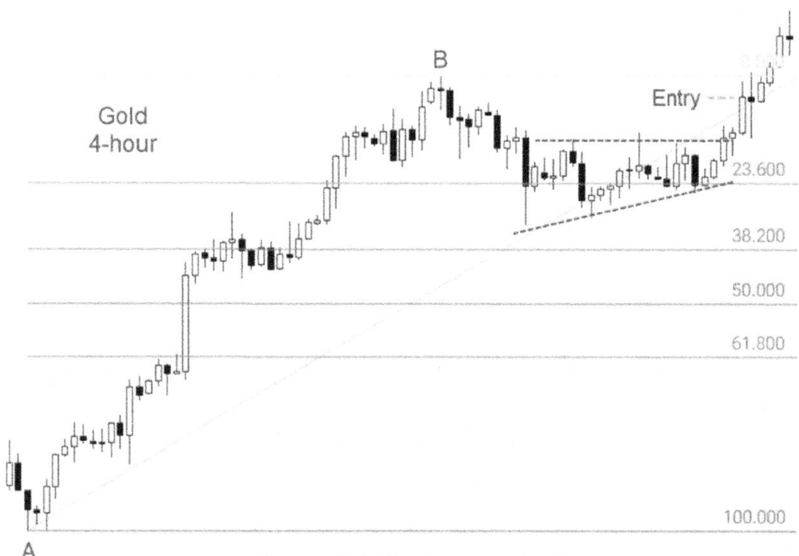

Figure 5.4: Trade example 10

Let us move on to the next example, once again using the gold market on the 4-hour timeframe.

First, let us establish the broader context. Similar to the previous example, gold had already experienced a strong bullish expansion beforehand, and what we are observing in Figure 5.4 is another continuation phase developing within that larger uptrend.

More broadly speaking, the strategy discussed in this chapter tends to appear more frequently in strongly trending markets. In contrast, if you recall the earlier strategies built around the Fibonacci 0.5–0.618 zone, those setups often emerged during transitional environments where the market was attempting to reverse from bearish to bullish conditions. The reason is quite intuitive. During potential reversals, the momentum of the pullback often aligns with the momentum of the previous dominant trend, naturally creating deeper retracements into the 0.5–0.618 equilibrium zone.

Now let us return to the chart itself. In this case, price only manages to retrace into the 0.236 Fibonacci level before entering a prolonged period of consolidation around that area. Bulls and Bears engage in an intense struggle inside the range. Every attempt by one side to move price is quickly answered by the other, gradually compressing the battle into a tightening structure. The upper boundary of the range remains relatively flat while the lower boundary slowly rises over time — a classic sign that buyers are beginning to gain positional advantage within the consolidation.

One important detail to emphasize here is the quality of the breakout candle itself. We are specifically looking for a decisive breakout candle, typically one with a sufficiently strong body and without an excessively long upper wick, exactly as illustrated at the entry point on the figure. A candle that merely pokes outside the consolidation with a weak body is generally considered insufficient. Such a breakout does not convincingly demonstrate that the dominant side has truly seized control of the battlefield.

Now let us see how price evolves after the breakout occurs.

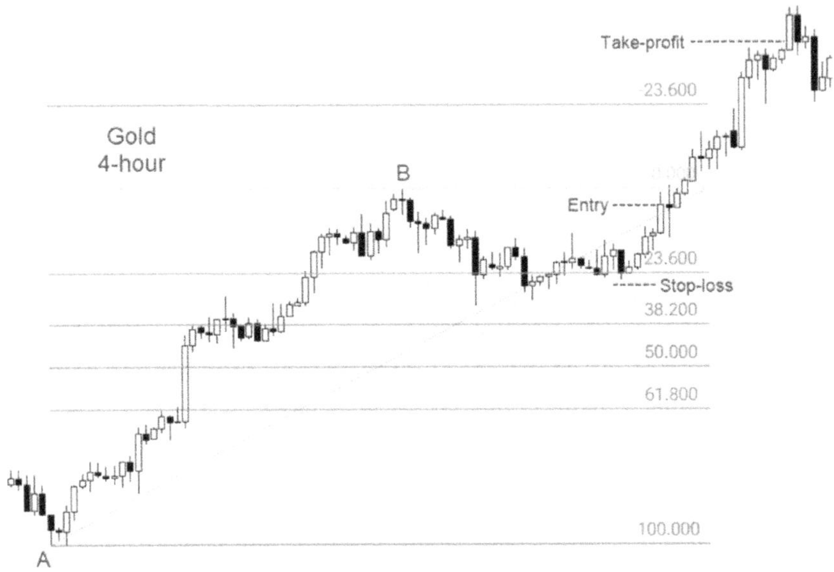

Figure 5.5: Trade example 10

In Figure 5.5, price encounters almost no meaningful difficulty in reaching the 2R target. Once again, the compressed structure with gradually rising lows provides us with a logical and efficient stop-loss placement, while the breakout candle itself remains both strong and balanced enough to deliver a high-quality entry.

Some readers may wonder whether entering at the close of the breakout candle is still justified given how close price already is to swing high B — a previous defensive stronghold of the Bears. This is a valid concern, and my answer comes largely from statistical observation accumulated through extensive trading experience: yes, the trade can still be taken confidently in this situation.

The reasoning is similar to the previous example. Although swing high B does represent a bearish defensive zone, it is not strong enough to invalidate the setup entirely. The evidence lies in the retracement behavior itself. Price only produced a shallow pullback before attempting continuation, and the retracement unfolded in a relatively gradual and controlled manner. This suggests that while selling pressure certainly exists, the Bears do not possess overwhelming strength in this environment. More importantly, the broader market context remains strongly trending, which gives us additional reason to expect that price can successfully break beyond the Fibonacci 0% level and continue the bullish expansion.

If we examine the price action in Figure 5.5 more carefully, we can also notice subtle hesitation during the two candles immediately following the breakout candle. Those candles reveal that sellers are still attempting to apply pressure near the previous swing high. However, the Bulls gradually absorb that resistance, force the Bears backward step by step, and ultimately overcome the resistance zone without major difficulty.

Trade Example 11

In this example, I want to show you how a trade that initially appears to be failing can sometimes be transformed into a winning trade through a simple but extremely practical trading technique. And once again, we will continue using the gold market as our example.

At this point, some of you are probably wondering why so many examples throughout this chapter involve gold. The reason is fairly straightforward: gold is an asset that tends to produce strong price movement and performs exceptionally well during highly trending market conditions. Its momentum characteristics make it particularly suitable for demonstrating the type of continuation setups discussed in this chapter. But that certainly does not mean these strategies apply only to gold. The concepts and techniques presented here are designed to work across virtually all tradable markets and asset classes, including currencies, stocks, indices, cryptocurrencies, and commodities alike.

Now let us move on to the next gold example on the 4-hour timeframe.

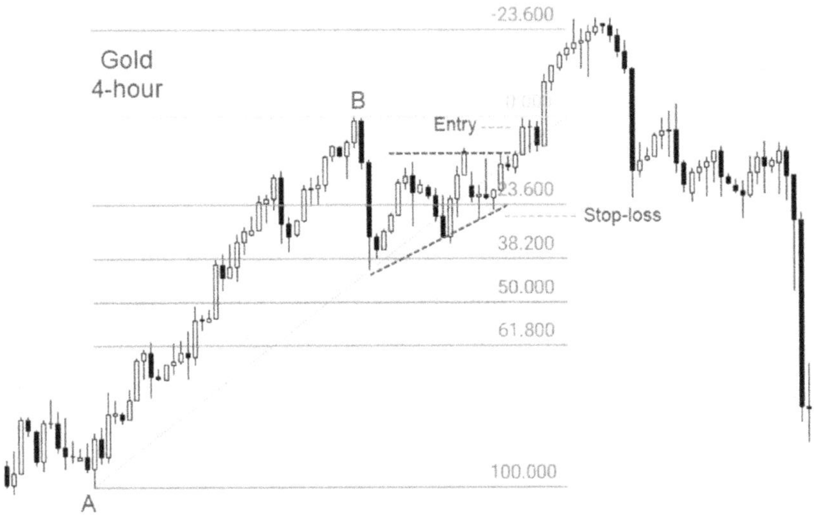

Figure 5.6: Trade example 11

Before the price action shown in Figure 5.6 began unfolding, the market had already gone through an exceptionally extended uptrend — perfectly reflecting the nature of a highly trending environment. In fact, the move displayed on this chart represents the final bullish expansion before the strong bearish decline that later appears on the right side of the figure.

The A–B impulse wave is the movement we use to project our Fibonacci levels. Compared to the earlier examples in this chapter, price retraces somewhat deeper this time, reaching the 0.382 Fibonacci level before finding support. From that moment onward, a compression structure immediately begins forming around the retracement zone. The highs remain relatively equal while the lows rise progressively higher, creating a textbook compression pattern. The eventual breakout candle escaping the structure also appears highly convincing: the body is large enough to demonstrate strong bullish momentum, yet still balanced enough to avoid extending excessively far away from the consolidation itself.

At first glance, everything seems ideal. The setup appears clean, the structure is organized, and the breakout is decisive. It looks exactly like the type of continuation trade we want to participate in.

And yet, despite the strong breakout above swing high B, the Bulls begin losing momentum shortly afterward. Instead of accelerating higher, price starts producing a series of small-bodied candles lacking follow-through momentum. The market hesitates. Then sellers suddenly return aggressively, reversing the move and eventually driving price down into the stop-loss zone.

This is an important reminder that losing trades are unavoidable in trading, no matter how carefully the preparation and analysis are performed. Even strong setups can fail. However, in certain situations, there are still ways to recover an edge from what initially appears to be a losing trade — sometimes through something surprisingly simple.

And that technique is familiar: move down to a lower timeframe.

So now let us examine what was actually happening beneath the surface on the 1-hour chart.

Figure 5.7: Trade example 11

What do we notice once we shift down to the 1-hour timeframe? A great deal of structural similarity, right? The same consolidation zone still exists — only now it is revealed through a larger number of candles. The highs remain relatively equal, while the three successive lows continue sloping upward clearly, once again reflecting the gradual dominance of the Bulls inside the contested area.

However, there is one extremely important detail that remains invisible on the 4-hour chart — and it becomes the true hidden gem of Figure 5.7. It is the smaller highlighted consolidation zone inside the larger structure.

This smaller range consists of nine candles tightly compressed together, representing an intense but localized battle between Bulls and Bears. In a sense, it is a consolidation nested inside a larger consolidation. And the critical detail is this: the upper boundary of the smaller range aligns almost perfectly with the upper boundary of the larger structure. That means when price eventually breaks through the smaller range, it simultaneously breaks through the larger compression zone as well — a double-layer breakout effect.

This becomes the key advantage of analyzing the setup on the 1-hour chart. The actual entry price itself does not differ dramatically compared to the 4-hour setup, but the stop-loss placement changes completely. Instead of positioning the stop-loss beneath the 0.236 Fibonacci level as in Figure 5.6 — which created a trade unable to achieve a proper 2R target before reversing — we can now place the stop directly beneath the smaller consolidation structure.

In other words, the distance between entry and stop-loss becomes significantly tighter, but importantly, this tighter stop is not arbitrary. It is supported by clear structural reasoning and still provides sufficient protection against normal market fluctuations. On top of that, lower-timeframe analysis often allows traders to participate slightly earlier than they otherwise could on higher timeframes alone.

As the chart later shows, price eventually rallies upward and reaches the 2R target cleanly.

I truly hope that through your own trading journey, you develop the habit of studying charts on lower timeframes regularly. It can become an incredibly valuable skill — far more valuable than most traders initially realize.

Trade Example 12

The final example in this chapter carries an important message about one of the most critical elements in trading: expectations.

To develop a more realistic understanding of the market, I want you to recognize that the examples shown throughout this book do not fully represent what real trading feels like day after day. The setups presented here are carefully selected to illustrate the concepts clearly and teach the logic behind the strategies. And to be fair, these types of high-quality setups absolutely do exist in live markets. In fact, if you remain patient and disciplined enough, you will encounter them repeatedly throughout your trading journey, often appearing in slightly different forms that still follow the same underlying principles.

But the market does not always behave this cleanly.

Sometimes unexpected news events inject chaos into price action. The market suddenly explodes violently in both directions, and your trade gets stopped out almost immediately despite the setup initially looking excellent. Other times, a market that previously displayed extremely strong momentum suddenly loses energy right after your entry, failing to continue the trend the way you expected. And occasionally, price simply refuses to behave logically at all. There are trades where you genuinely cannot find a satisfying explanation for why the market failed.

That is normal.

After years of trading, I can honestly say there are still many losing trades I do not attempt to overanalyze anymore. They are simply part of the game. Trading, at least from my perspective, is ultimately a game of probabilities. If the strategy itself possesses a genuine edge and the trader executing it possesses the necessary discipline, patience, and emotional control, profitability takes care of itself over the long run.

Now let us move on to the following example.

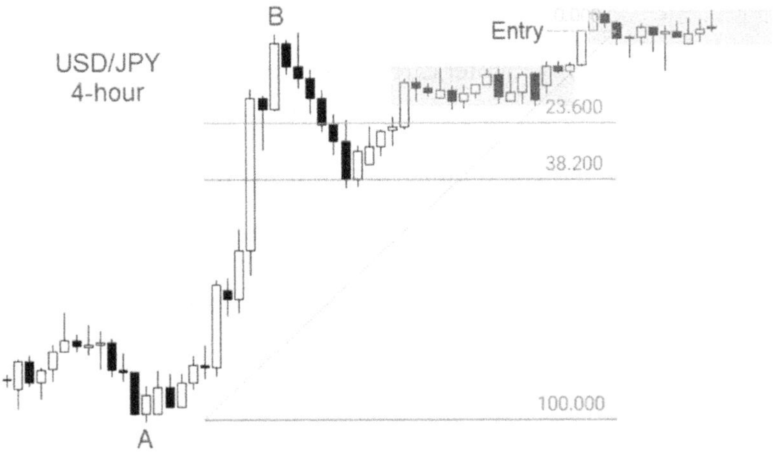

Figure 5.8: Trade Example 12

Figure 5.8 presents the USD/JPY 4-hour chart in a clear high-trending environment. The A–B impulse wave is easy to identify and serves as the foundation for projecting our Fibonacci levels. Price retraces precisely into the 0.382 Fibonacci level, but what stands out is the character of the pullback itself. The retracement unfolds with relatively strong downward momentum, producing six consecutive bearish candles, with the final candle displaying the largest body of the entire decline. For a shallow price retracement, this type of momentum is not particularly common — shallow pullbacks more often unwind gradually rather than with this degree of bearish conviction. It remains a visible sign of strong commitment from the Bears.

And yet, buyers respond immediately. The Bulls gradually lift price back above the 0.236 Fibonacci level, where the market then begins forming its first consolidation structure. This contested range extends across dozens of 4-hour candles, creating a prolonged period of compression and hesitation between both sides.

Eventually, what appears to be a textbook breakout setup emerges. A strong bullish candle breaks decisively above the consolidation zone with clear momentum and without any significant rejection wick, giving us what seems like an ideal continuation entry.

But here is the interesting detail: the entry price itself sits almost exactly at the same level as the previous swing high B.

Structurally, we already understand that swing high B should naturally create at least some resistance pressure because it represents a previous defensive zone from the Bears. However, since the preceding retracement remained relatively shallow within the Fibonacci structure, the expectation under this strategy is that price should possess enough momentum to break through B and continue the bullish expansion.

So what happens in this situation?

The reality is that at the moment we enter the trade, we still cannot truly know how the price action will unfold afterward. Everything ultimately rests on one word: expectation.

We expect price to continue higher and eventually reach the projected take-profit target, but the exact way the market behaves afterward can never be known with certainty. As traders, our role is not to predict the future perfectly. Our role is to observe, and determine which side currently holds the higher probability. And that assessment usually comes from two different layers of observation.

- Is the momentum beginning to struggle?

This becomes the first layer.

On Figure 5.8, the candle immediately following the breakout remains bullish, but its body is already smaller than the breakout candle itself. Then, instead of accelerating upward cleanly, price begins forming another consolidation structure. At this stage, we can see that the Bulls are no longer able to push the market higher immediately. However, there is still an important detail worth noticing: the new consolidation zone forms above the previous consolidation range.

This is actually a scenario we have already encountered multiple times throughout the book. Structurally, as long as the market continues building higher contested zones rather than collapsing downward, the broader advantage still technically belongs to the buyers. One more successful breakout to the upside would likely reestablish bullish momentum and confirm continuation once again.

So how do we answer the question: "Is momentum encountering difficulty?"

Yes — it clearly is.

But at this stage, the story is still unresolved. The market has shown hesitation, yet the overall structure has not broken down completely. For now, we continue waiting and observing.

- Is the momentum beginning to move against our expectation?

This second layer of observation is more serious because it forces us to evaluate whether the market is starting to behave in direct opposition to the scenario we originally anticipated. Our expectation is clear: we want to see price break upward and continue the dominant trend. But is the actual price action still supporting that expectation?

Figure 5.9: Trade Example 12

On Figure 5.9, price does not break upward. Instead, it breaks down beneath the consolidation structure. And importantly, the breakout occurs through a strong bearish full-body candle with virtually no wick at all — a sign that buyers offered almost no meaningful resistance during the decline. Even though the candle itself has not yet broken below the absolute lowest wick inside the broader price range, the message from the momentum has already changed significantly.

This type of candle matters because it reveals more than simple hesitation. It suggests that the dominant side — the Bulls in this case — may no longer possess the same level of control that existed earlier in the setup. The market is no longer merely struggling to continue upward. It is beginning to push actively against the original expectation itself.

So how do we answer the second question: "Is momentum now moving against our expectation?"

At this stage, the answer becomes yes.

Now let us observe how the price action develops afterward.

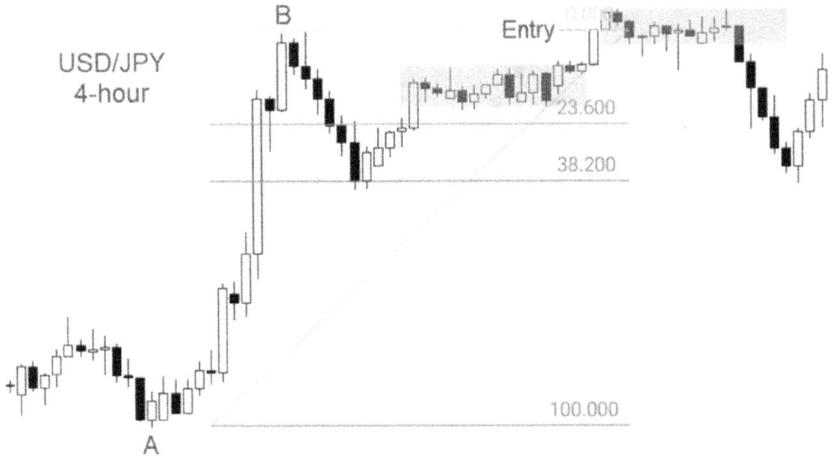

Figure 5.10: Trade Example 12

Price continues declining and eventually sweeps beneath both of the earlier consolidation zones before finally bouncing upward again. Our trade gets stopped out.

Some traders may argue that entering at a price level equal to the previous swing high — point B — already carried additional risk from the beginning. Others, especially readers familiar with some of my other books, may interpret this move as a liquidity sweep before the market eventually resumes the dominant trend afterward. Both perspectives are understandable.

But personally, I prefer not to overcomplicate the strategy.

The reality is that every trading strategy is built upon its own analytical framework and internal logic. Different strategies interpret the same market behavior differently. Because of that, my conclusion here remains relatively simple: this is just part of the game.

There are losing trades we can explain clearly in hindsight, and there are others where the explanation remains far less obvious. But constantly trying to justify or intellectually "solve" every losing trade is not the most important part of trading anyway. Trading is ultimately a game of probabilities, not certainty.

What matters far more is maintaining consistency in how we execute the strategy itself. My primary focus is always to respect the rules of my system as faithfully as possible, then review the strategy only after a sufficiently long period of execution — when enough data, experience, and perspective have accumulated to allow for a deeper and more meaningful evaluation of the edge itself.

Trading is ultimately a game of probabilities. Regardless of which factor — or combination of factors — influences your trades, if that influence produces a positive outcome across a sufficiently large sample size (at least a few hundred trades), then you possess a long-term edge. And if it does not, then you do not.

That is why individual wins and losses carry very little meaning by themselves. A single trade cannot validate or invalidate a strategy. Because of that, one of the most important skills in trading is learning how to regulate your expectations and emotions appropriately — neither becoming excessively euphoric after wins nor emotionally crushed after losses.

And with that, we arrive at the end of this chapter.

The strategy presented in this chapter does not require us to react faster than the market — that would be impossible. What it requires is the ability to recognize the type of flow currently dominating the market, then patiently wait for the precise moment when the consolidation structure releases its stored energy so we can align ourselves with the strongest current already moving beneath the surface — while still maintaining disciplined self-management throughout the process.

In the next chapter, we will dive deeper into the art of taking profits and managing capital while trading advanced Fibonacci strategies.

CHAPTER 6: TAKE-PROFIT AND TRADE MANAGEMENT STRATEGIES

With that, we have now completed the four advanced entry strategies combining Fibonacci analysis with price action — strategies distilled from more than two decades of my own trading experience. These setups demand a high level of confluence, which naturally means they do not appear very often. But that rarity is precisely what gives them greater strength. Whenever all the required conditions align together, we know we are operating from a stronger foundation than most ordinary entries found in the market.

The philosophy of "trading with your ass" — patiently waiting for the right scenario instead of trading out of boredom or restlessness — gradually shapes a trading style that is both structured and internally consistent. Once this mindset becomes deeply internalized, you no longer need to stare obsessively at charts hunting for signals or mentally exhausting yourself comparing whether one setup is slightly better than another. The process of optimizing entries through Fibonacci logic and the ongoing battle between Bulls and Bears slowly becomes something natural in the way you interpret the market — simple, consistent, and effective.

However, no matter how strong an entry strategy or stop-loss framework may be, a trading system can never become complete without the equally important component that follows afterward: take-profit execution and trade management. And in trading, this is often the hardest part of all — not because the techniques themselves are overly complicated, but because of the psychological pressure involved.

Before entering a trade, you hold no position. Emotionally, the mind remains relatively neutral. But the moment a position is opened, everything changes. From that point onward, you exist in one of only two states: either floating in profit or floating in loss.

And the uncomfortable truth is that regardless of which state you are in, emotions inevitably begin creeping into the decision-making process. The larger the unrealized profit or loss becomes, the more noticeable the emotional influence grows. If emotions are allowed to take control, all the effort spent patiently finding a high-quality entry beforehand can quickly become meaningless. A winning trade can turn into a losing one. A small controlled loss can spiral into a much larger disaster.

That is precisely why I chose to dedicate an entire chapter specifically to take-profit execution and trade management rather than scattering the discussion across earlier chapters. In many ways, the way a trader manages exits reveals far more about their long-term potential than the entry itself. Entries may create opportunities, but trade management is often what determines whether those opportunities ultimately translate into consistent profitability.

The concepts shared in this chapter are not overly complicated. In fact, most of them are deceptively simple. But when applied properly and consistently, their impact can be greater than many traders initially expect.

At the same time, it is important to understand that the art of taking profits is not built around a single universal formula that works perfectly for everyone. Trade management is deeply connected to personality and trading style. A conservative trader will naturally make different decisions compared to a more aggressive trader, even when both are analyzing the exact same setup.

Throughout this chapter, I will present multiple scenarios and approaches for you to study and consider. But honestly, discovering which style truly fits you can only happen through your own trading experience and personal reflection over time. That process may take patience — but it is absolutely worth it.

Taking Profit at the Nearest Key Level

Why prioritize taking profit at the nearest key level? The logic is actually very straightforward: that level represents the defensive territory of the opposing side, meaning price is likely to encounter significant pressure there.

Take a long position as an example. After entering the trade, price begins moving in the expected direction and eventually approaches a resistance zone — an area where sellers previously managed to defend successfully in the past. When the market returns to that same area, a very real possibility emerges: the Bears may already be waiting there again, ready to challenge the bullish momentum and slow the advance.

Because of that, taking profit at the nearest resistance level is often one of the safest and most structurally justified approaches available. It aligns directly with the underlying logic of market battles that we have discussed throughout this book.

That said, the decision surrounding profit-taking at a key level is not always completely straightforward. Several additional factors can influence how we manage the trade once price approaches those areas, as we will explore below.

The Strength of Key Levels

Not all key levels carry the same weight. In practice, there are two major factors that help us evaluate how significant a key level truly is.

The first factor is the strength of the price reaction that previously emerged from that level — specifically its slope and duration. If price once collapsed sharply, aggressively, and over a prolonged distance after touching a resistance zone, that is usually evidence of a strong key level. It suggests that sellers were able to overwhelm buyers decisively and seize control of the market with little resistance. On the other hand, if price only drifted downward gradually or produced a relatively shallow pullback afterward, then the bearish pressure at that level was likely less dominant.

The second factor is the timeframe on which the key level was formed. A resistance or support zone identified on the daily or weekly timeframe naturally carries far greater structural importance than a level visible only on lower intraday charts such as the hourly timeframe.

The stronger a key level becomes, the greater the probability that price will encounter intense conflict between buyers and sellers once it reaches that area again. In those situations, taking full or partial profits becomes something traders should seriously consider. Conversely, when a key level appears only moderately significant, we gain more justification for expecting price to eventually break through and continue trending further. In those cases, the profit-taking strategy itself may become more flexible and depend heavily on the trader's individual style and risk tolerance.

The Distance Between Entry and Key Levels

The distance between your entry point and the nearest key level is an extremely important variable to evaluate before deciding whether a trade is worth taking. Personally, the minimum reference threshold I recommend is around 1.5R — this is generally the lowest level at which a trade still maintains meaningful reward-to-risk potential.

Depending on whether the nearest key level is relatively close to the entry or located much further away, the way we approach trade management can differ significantly.

If the Nearest Key Level Is Too Close — Below 1.5R

For conservative traders, if the nearby key level is not considered particularly strong, the trade may still be worth considering. However, instead of taking profit directly at that nearby level, the idea is to ignore it and aim for the next more distant key level instead — especially when applying the momentum-based strategies discussed in Chapter 5. On the other hand, if the nearby key level is structurally strong, the better decision is often to avoid the trade entirely.

For aggressive traders, the approach becomes more flexible. If the nearby key level is relatively weak, the trade can still be taken while ignoring that level and targeting a more distant objective instead — ideally no less than 2R. If the nearby key level is strong, the trade may still remain valid, but partial profit-taking becomes worth considering. In that case, a portion of the position can be closed at the nearby key level to secure gains, while the remaining portion is left open in case price successfully breaks through and continues trending further.

If the Nearest Key Level Is Far Away — Beyond 3R

A large amount of open price space is generally a favorable condition, but it might require a more active approach to trade management. In these situations, the approach depends largely on the trader's individual style. For more conservative traders, securing profits somewhere in the 2R to 3R range is a reasonable and disciplined objective. For those with a more aggressive approach, the position can be left open beyond that threshold, with the final decision guided by the evolving price action as the trade develops.

Several warning signs become important to watch for during this process: candle bodies gradually shrinking in size, increasing appearance of rejection wicks against the trade direction, price entering prolonged consolidation without making further progress, or bearish breakouts developing after a consolidation phase. When these behaviors begin appearing, they often suggest that momentum is weakening, and that may become the appropriate moment to consider taking profit rather than continuing to hold the position indefinitely.

Taking Profit Using a Fixed Reward:Risk Ratio

The second take-profit method — and also one of my personal favorites — is using a fixed Reward:Risk ratio. The idea is simple: the moment you enter a trade, you already know in advance how much profit you are aiming for relative to the amount of risk you are willing to accept.

For example, after entering a position and placing the stop-loss beneath the consolidation structure, if your chosen fixed R:R ratio is 2, you simply measure the distance between the entry and the stop-loss, then multiply that distance by two to determine the take-profit target. Once price reaches that level, the trade closes automatically and the profit is secured. This is the method I used frequently throughout the shallow-retracement continuation strategies discussed in Chapter 5, especially in situations where identifying a nearby meaningful key level from recent price history was difficult.

The greatest advantage of this method is its simplicity. It is easy to monitor, easy to execute, and highly effective at reducing emotional interference. You no longer need to constantly stare at the chart wondering, "Should I hold longer or take profit now?" because the entire plan has already been defined beforehand. Many traders refer to this as a "set and forget" approach — place the trade, define the risk and target, then allow the market to do the rest. Because of its consistency and emotional stability, this style of trade management is particularly suitable for newer traders or anyone trying to develop a more systematic trading mindset.

Of course, this method is not a magical formula that guarantees success — nothing in trading can do that. There will still be winning trades and losing trades. The objective is simply to maintain a statistical edge over a sufficiently large sample size. Sometimes price will come very close to the take-profit target before reversing all the way back to the stop-loss. We must accept that. Other times, price will continue trending far beyond the target after the trade has already been closed. That is also part of the game. But by consistently following a predefined plan, we protect ourselves from emotional decision-making and create the stability necessary for long-term survival and profitability.

Why Reward:Risk = 2?

This question deserves a direct answer, because an R:R ratio of 2 is not a random number chosen arbitrarily.

The first reason is probability mathematics. With a R:R ratio of 2, you only need to win slightly more than 33% of your trades to break even. Anything above that already produces positive expectancy over the long run. This threshold is realistic enough to survive even during difficult market periods. When losing streaks inevitably occur, the account is still protected from eroding too quickly.

The second reason is trading psychology. An R:R ratio of 1 requires a win rate above 50% just to remain profitable — and that creates enormous psychological pressure. Many traders begin breaking discipline after several consecutive losses because they feel constant pressure to maintain a high win rate. An R:R ratio of 2 creates enough breathing room psychologically to accept losses without emotionally destabilizing the trader, while still providing sufficient reward to maintain confidence in following the system consistently.

The third reason is more personal. Over the course of backtesting thousands of trades, 2R emerged consistently as a threshold that strikes the right balance between ambition and realism. Targets beyond that — such as 3R or 4R — are certainly achievable in favorable conditions, but they also introduce a meaningful risk of price reversing before the target is reached, particularly in noisy or choppy market environments. A 2R objective, by contrast, is demanding enough to produce meaningful results over time, yet attainable enough that the trade does not need perfect conditions to succeed.

Of course, when market conditions are especially favorable — strong momentum, abundant open space ahead, and no significant opposing key levels nearby — then targeting 3R or even larger moves can absolutely become a valid consideration. But overall, R:R = 2 remains the baseline standard I personally recommend because it represents one of the healthiest balances between practicality, consistency, and long-term performance.

Hybrid Take-Profit Method

The final take-profit approach discussed in this chapter is the hybrid method — and in many ways, it is also the most flexible of the three approaches.

Instead of closing the entire position at a single predefined target, the hybrid method divides profit-taking into at least two stages: one portion is closed early to secure realized profit, while the remaining portion is left open to capture the larger trend extensions that the market occasionally provides.

A fixed Reward:Risk model certainly has important advantages — simplicity, discipline, and emotional neutrality. But its limitation is equally clear: the trade is always exited at the same point regardless of whether the market still possesses strong momentum afterward. Long directional moves, extended trends, and multi-level expansions become impossible to fully participate in if we always close the entire position at 2R and simply watch price continue moving afterward without us.

The hybrid method attempts to solve this problem without forcing us to expose the entire position to unpredictable market conditions. Part of the position is secured at a logical target with clear structural justification, helping protect profits and reduce psychological pressure. The remaining portion is then allowed to be guided by the market itself, with price action analysis helping determine the most appropriate exit point later on.

Depending on the specific market context, the implementation of this approach can vary significantly — which is why I divide it into the three scenarios discussed below.

First scenario

The first scenario occurs when a strong key level is located very close to the entry point — too close for us to comfortably place the entire take-profit target there while still maintaining an attractive reward-to-risk ratio, yet important enough that ignoring it completely would also be dangerous.

In this situation, instead of choosing only one option — either taking full profit at the nearby key level or ignoring it entirely and targeting something further away — we combine both approaches simultaneously. We close 50% of the position once price reaches the nearby key level, while keeping the remaining 50% open and aiming toward the next more distant key level. The objective is to ensure that when averaging both exits together, the overall trade still achieves at least a 1.5R return — the minimum threshold required for the trade to remain meaningful from a Reward:Risk perspective.

This approach solves a very common dilemma many traders face in practice. If the nearby key level is too close, taking full profit there often produces an unattractive R:R profile. But completely ignoring the level creates the risk that price may reverse sharply before ever reaching the more distant target. By securing partial profits at the nearby resistance, we protect part of the gain before price encounters a potentially difficult barrier, while still preserving the opportunity to benefit if the market successfully breaks through and continues trending further.

After taking partial profit at the nearby key level, if overall market conditions remain favorable — price movement stays orderly, volatility remains controlled, and no major news events are approaching — we may consider moving the stop-loss to breakeven in order to eliminate downside risk entirely on the remaining portion of the trade.

However, if the market produces more volatility, it is often better to leave the stop-loss at its original location and allow the trade sufficient room to breathe. Getting stopped out at breakeven by a short-term liquidity spike while the broader trend remains perfectly intact is an unnecessary frustration that can often be avoided through a bit more patience and flexibility.

Second Scenario

The second scenario occurs when the nearest key level sits at an ideal distance from the entry — far enough that closing the full position there would naturally produce an R:R ratio somewhere between 2R and 3R. This is generally one of the most comfortable environments for trading, and it is also where the hybrid method becomes especially powerful in a different way.

Instead of taking full profit once price reaches that key level, we close only 50% of the position there in order to secure a meaningful portion of realized profit. The remaining 50% is then left without a fixed take-profit target and allowed to be guided by the market itself. The purpose here is not greed. It is simply an acknowledgment of a basic market reality: sometimes trends extend far beyond what we could reasonably anticipate at the beginning of the trade, and if we always close the entire position at the first target, we completely lose the opportunity to participate in those larger moves.

For the remaining portion, we continue monitoring the evolving price action to identify an appropriate exit point — similar to the momentum-weakening signals discussed earlier in this chapter. These warning signs may include candle bodies gradually shrinking, increasing appearance of rejection wicks against the trend direction, or price beginning to consolidate without making further progress before eventually breaking back against the position afterward. Once those signals begin appearing consistently, it often becomes the appropriate moment to close the remaining portion of the trade.

Just like in the first scenario, after securing 50% profit at the key level, we may consider moving the stop-loss on the remaining portion up to breakeven — but only when market conditions remain orderly and stable. If unusual volatility, erratic price behavior, or major upcoming news events are present, it is often wiser to leave the original stop-loss untouched and allow the trade sufficient room to continue developing naturally.

Third scenario

The third scenario occurs when there is no obvious key level ahead — or when the available key levels are projected from price action far back in history, making them less reliable as immediate reference points for anticipating strong reactions. This situation appears most frequently when applying the shallow Fibonacci retracement strategies discussed in the previous chapter, particularly during high-trending market conditions where price still has a large amount of open space ahead.

In this case, we close 50% of the position at a fixed 2R target — a profit objective grounded in clear mathematical logic rather than dependent on interpreting future price structure. This portion becomes the "secured profit," protected regardless of whatever the market chooses to do afterward.

For the remaining 50%, instead of using a fixed take-profit target, we transition into reading price action dynamically in order to determine the exit. There is no rigid formula here. We simply observe how price behaves after surpassing the 2R level: does momentum remain strong, do candle bodies continue closing decisively, or are early signs of weakening beginning to appear? Once those warning signals emerge — shrinking candle bodies, growing rejection wicks against the trend direction, or consolidation that fails to make further progress — that is typically the moment to close the remaining portion of the trade.

Just like in the previous two scenarios, after securing 50% profit at 2R, moving the stop-loss on the remaining portion up to breakeven becomes a reasonable option to consider — especially in high-trending environments where price often moves in relatively orderly expansions. However, if market conditions become unstable or major news events are approaching, it is usually wiser to leave the original stop-loss untouched in order to avoid being shaken out prematurely by short-term volatility spikes or unnecessary noise.

Trading does not end the moment you press the entry button. It ends the moment you exit the trade — and the way you exit is ultimately what determines whether all the analysis, patience, and discipline that came beforehand are truly transformed into meaningful results.

The three take-profit methods discussed in this chapter represent three different approaches, each suited to different market environments and different trader personalities. Taking profit at the nearest key level provides structurally grounded safety. The fixed Reward:Risk method provides discipline and consistency. The hybrid method offers flexibility, allowing us to capture more of what the market is genuinely willing to give.

Understanding who you are as a trader — whether you are naturally conservative or aggressive, patient or emotionally reactive — becomes the foundation for choosing the right approach and sticking with it long enough for the edge to reveal itself over time.

A wise leaf does not only know how to enter the current. It also knows when to let go — when to allow the river to carry it further downstream, and when to stop before being pulled into the whirlpool. That is the art this chapter hopes to pass on to you.

CHAPTER 7: UNCONSCIOUS REFLEXES

There is a question that almost every trader or investor eventually asks themselves at some point — whether after one year in the market or five: why is it that we can study countless trading patterns, understand market psychology inside out, read book after book about discipline and risk management… yet the moment real money is on the line and the chart starts moving, all of that knowledge suddenly disappears?

Where does our rational thinking go at that moment?

When price approaches the stop-loss, you already know exactly what you are supposed to do. You know the loss should be cut. But somehow your hand refuses to stay still. Instead of letting price hit the stop naturally, you move the stop-loss slightly further away, hoping the market will turn back. And when the trade finally moves in your favor, long before price reaches the target, you rush to close the position early out of fear that the market might reverse and take the profit away from you.

Most people will simply tell you that you lack discipline. But I want to offer you a deeper perspective than that: you are struggling because you are trying to trade through conscious thought, while the market ultimately demands that you trade through reflex.

Look at real life for a moment and you will begin to understand the power of unconscious reflex.

When your hand accidentally touches a burning hot pot, you pull it away instantly. You do not pause to think: "This is hot… should I move my hand away or not?" The reaction happens before conscious thought even has time to appear. Or imagine driving on the road when another car suddenly cuts in front of you. You slam on the brakes immediately. You do not stop to analyze what brand the car is, how fast it is moving, or whether you should brake gently or aggressively. If you tried to consciously process all of that first, the accident would already have happened.

Trading and investing work the same way.

During moments of extreme volatility, during violent reversals and fast-moving price action, conscious thinking alone will almost never react quickly enough. The highest level of trading is not about how intelligent a trader is. It is about whether that trader has trained a sufficiently sharp unconscious reflex system — one capable of protecting them from danger while still allowing them to seize opportunity when it appears.

Inside every one of us exists an unconscious machine. It operates 24/7, constantly trying to protect us.

But here lies the problem: financial markets are not a natural environment. The very instincts and unconscious survival reflexes that help us function in real life often become the exact things that destroy our trading accounts.

And unfortunately, most people are being driven by the wrong unconscious reflexes without even realizing it. Ask yourself honestly whether you recognize any of the following patterns.

The unconscious reflex of curiosity. You constantly search for a new method. Today you see someone making money with SMC, so you rush to study SMC. Tomorrow someone posts profits using Ichimoku, and suddenly you abandon everything to chase Ichimoku instead. Your unconscious mind keeps searching for a holy grail — something new to temporarily soothe your insecurity and escape boredom — rather than staying focused long enough to master one thing deeply.

The reflex of fear after repeated pain. After experiencing enough suffering from the market — blown accounts, painful losing streaks, emotional exhaustion — your brain's natural defense mechanism slowly begins treating entering a trade itself as dangerous. And the result is hesitation. Even when a textbook-quality setup appears right in front of you, you still freeze. You tell yourself, "Maybe I should wait for one more candle just to be safe." Then price takes off without you, regret kicks in, and eventually you chase the move at the worst possible moment. That is the reflex of a wounded animal, not the reflex of a trained marksman.

The reflex of greed and refusing to accept losses. When a trade goes against you, your ego struggles to accept being wrong. Your unconscious mind whispers: "If I close the trade now, the loss becomes real. Just hold a little longer — maybe it will come back." In that moment, you are using primal survival instinct to fight against the probabilistic nature of the market itself.

We are living inside a strange paradox: using conscious reasoning to justify mistakes created by the unconscious mind. We think we are calmly analyzing the market, but in reality, many times we are simply becoming servants to emotional impulses we do not fully control.

To become consistently profitable, you must learn how to reprogram this internal machinery. You must use conscious effort to build a new set of unconscious reflexes — the reflexes of a professional trader.

There is a famous quote from Bruce Lee that captures this idea perfectly: "I fear not the man who has practiced 10,000 kicks once, but I fear the man who has practiced one kick 10,000 times." Why practice the same kick 10,000 times? Because when the opponent attacks, he no longer needs to consciously think about how to react. His leg moves automatically into the correct position. The strike comes out naturally, precisely toward the opening. At that point, conscious thought has stepped aside and allowed unconscious reflex to take over.

Trading and investing require reaching a very similar state. When the setup matches your rules, you execute. No hesitation. No hope. No fear.

So how do we transform a dry set of rules written on paper into a reflex embedded deep inside us? There are three foundational pillars that completely changed the way I approached trading.

Pillar One: Simplicity and Reflex

Reflex can only become fast when the process itself is simple. If your trading system contains too many conditions, the brain is forced into a slow comparison process every time a setup appears. At that point, it is no longer reflex — it becomes analytical processing. And just like most traders in the beginning, we become fascinated by countless indicators, believing that the more tools we add, the better our system becomes. But when an entry finally appears, we freeze because we are busy checking each condition one by one. That is not reflex anymore.

Choose one pattern. One market structure. One entry scenario.

Study it and observe it so many times that eventually you only need three seconds looking at a chart to know whether a valid setup exists or not. If the setup does not match your rules, you close the chart and walk away peacefully without frustration or attachment — that is reflex. And if the setup does match your rules, you execute the trade decisively like a machine: no hope, no fear. Whether the trade wins or loses belongs to probability. Your job is simply to execute the reflex you have trained.

Pillar Two: Backtesting — Sharpening the Blade in the Dark

Backtesting is not merely about discovering a strategy's win rate — that is only the surface level. The deeper purpose of backtesting is to retrain the brain itself. Once you have seen the same setup win one hundred times and lose fifty times throughout historical data, your mind slowly begins accepting losses as something normal. It understands that as long as the rules are followed consistently, the edge still remains profitable over time — unless you sabotage it yourself through random impulsive trades. At that point, the reflexive fear of losing begins fading away, replaced instead by an acceptance of probability. Trading psychology no longer feels like an enemy you must constantly fight against. It simply becomes part of the environment you have learned to live within.

And if you want your backtesting to become truly meaningful, you need a tool capable of replaying historical price action as though you were trading live markets in real time. One platform I personally trust for this purpose is Forex Tester Online — a browser-based simulator that requires no installation and can be accessed from virtually any device. It provides tick-by-tick historical data spanning more than twenty years, allowing you to observe the internal movement inside each candle rather than simply viewing completed candles after the fact. Combined with trade management tools, performance analytics, and even prop-firm style simulation environments, it turns backtesting into a far more structured and realistic training process.

You can access Forex Tester Online at frankmillertrading.com/backtest.

Pillar Three: Forced Discipline

At the beginning, discipline has to be enforced consciously. If the setup is not there, you do not take the trade. If the market spends the entire day without giving you a valid opportunity, you close the charts and move on with your life. It feels difficult at first — just like going to the gym. The first few weeks are painful. But eventually, you reach a point where not following your routine feels stranger than following it. That is when discipline stops being effort and starts becoming reflex.

And once that reflex is fully built, something powerful begins to happen: you are no longer trading alone. You are standing on the shoulders of a giant. That giant is not a bank, a hedge fund, or some mysterious institution. It is the trading system you have carved deep into your own unconscious mind through repetition and training.

Imagine this situation. A terrible piece of news hits the market. Price collapses violently. Everywhere around you, people are panicking. Some dump positions out of fear. Others blindly try to catch the bottom. Their decisions are being controlled entirely by emotion. Fear clouds their judgment, greed blinds their thinking.

But you sit there calmly.

Your unconscious reflex immediately recognizes the situation. You have seen this chaos before — not just in the market, but inside yourself. You remember what happens when emotions take over. You remember the pain of impulsive decisions. More importantly, you have already studied hundreds of similar situations through backtesting, journaling, and repetition. You know exactly what conditions must appear before the probability shifts back in your favor.

So you wait.

And when the market finally produces the same familiar setup you have practiced a thousand times before, your reflex takes over. No hesitation. No excitement. No fear. Your hand clicks the mouse calmly, almost automatically.

At that point, you no longer obsess over whether this individual trade will win or lose. That question no longer matters as much as it once did. What matters is that you executed your process correctly.

That is the moment you begin escaping the control of primitive instinct and move closer toward becoming a consistently profitable trader.

The journey from conscious effort to unconscious reflex does not happen overnight. It is a long process of slowly wearing down the ego and dismantling habits that may have been deeply rooted inside us for decades. If you currently feel exhausted, inconsistent, or lacking discipline, do not condemn yourself too harshly — it simply means you have not repeated the process enough times yet for the behavior to become truly automatic. The highest level of trading is not the ability to predict the future. It is reaching a state where, no matter what the market does, you already know what must be done — and you do it calmly, without fear, without hesitation, and without needing to think twice.

I sincerely wish you the patience to keep training, the discipline to keep refining your process, and eventually the ability to reach that state of unconscious reflex — not only in trading and investing, but in any skill you choose to dedicate yourself to mastering.

Before you leave, I'd like to ask a small favor.

HELP ANOTHER TRADER SUCCEED

"The best traders don't just learn from the market — they help others learn too."

If any part of this book resonated with your struggles, helped you see the market more clearly, or if the strategies shared here brought real value to your trading journey, I would truly appreciate an honest review from you.

There may be another trader somewhere out there, quietly struggling with the same questions you once had — and your review could be the thing that helps guide them forward in their own development.

People who share what they know often help others grow faster and feel more confident in their journey — which is why your words can make a real difference.

So I'm kindly asking you, as someone interested in trading and market analysis, to leave a quick review.

To help, just scan the QR code below to leave your review:

Thank you very much for your support.

Frank Miller.

CHECK OUT OTHER BOOKS

Scan this barcode to access my full collection of trading books- packed with proven methods, fresh insights, and powerful techniques to help you trade smarter and grow faster.	
Scan this barcode to stay updated when new books are released.	

Made in the USA
Monee, IL
16 September 2026

63296744R00075